Top Careers in Two Years

Business, Finance, and Government Administration

Titles in the *Top Careers in Two Years* Series

Top Careers in Two Years

Business, Finance, and Government Administration

By Celia W. Seupel

Ferguson Publishing
An imprint of Infobase Publishing

Top Careers in Two Years

Business, Finance, and Government Adminstration

Ferguson
An imprint of Infobase Publishing
132 West 31st Street
New York, NY 10001

ISBN-13: 978-0-8160-6899-9
ISBN-10: 0-8160-6899-2

Library of Congress Cataloging-in-Publication Data

Top careers in two years.
    v. cm.
    Includes index.
    Contents: v. 1. Food, agriculture, and natural resources / by Scott Gillam — v. 2. Construction and trades / Deborah Porterfield — v. 3. Communications and the arts / Claire Wyckoff — v. 4. Business, finance, and government administration / Celia W. Seupal — v. 5. Education and social services / Jessica Cohn — v. 6. Health care, medicine, and science / Deborah Porterfield — v. 7. Hospitality, human services, and tourism / Rowan Riley — v. 8. Computers and information technology / Claire Wyckoff — v. 9. Public safety, law, and security / Lisa Cornelio, Gail Eisenberg — v. 10. Manufacturing and transportation — v. 11. Retail, marketing, and sales / Paul Stinson.
    ISBN-13: 978-0-8160-6896-8 (v. 1 : hc : alk. paper)
    ISBN-10: 0-8160-6896-8 (v. 1 : hc : alk. paper)
    ISBN-13: 978-0-8160-6897-5 (v. 2 : hc : alk. paper)
    ISBN-10: 0-8160-6897-6 (v. 2 : hc. : alk. paper)
    ISBN-13: 978-0-8160-6898-2 (v. 3 : hc : alk. paper)
    ISBN-10: 0-8160-6898-4 (v. 3 : hc : alk. paper)
    ISBN-13: 978-0-8160-6899-9 (v. 4 : hc : alk. paper)
    ISBN-10: 0-8160-6899-2 (v. 4 : hc : alk. paper)
    ISBN-13: 978-0-8160-6900-2 (v. 5 : hc : alk. paper)
    ISBN-10: 0-8160-6900-X (v. 5 : hc : alk. paper)
    ISBN-13: 978-0-8160-6901-9 (v. 6 : hc : alk. paper)
    ISBN-10: 0-8160-6901-8 (v. 6 : hc : alk. paper)
    ISBN-13: 978-0-8160-6902-6 (v. 7 : hc : alk. paper)
    ISBN-10: 0-8160-6902-6 (v. 7 : hc : alk. paper)
    ISBN-13: 978-0-8160-6903-3 (v. 8 : hc : alk. paper)
    ISBN-10: 0-8160-6903-4 (v. 8 : hc : alk. paper)
    ISBN-13: 978-0-8160-6904-0 (v. 9 : hc : alk. paper)
    ISBN-10: 0-8160-6904-2 (v. 9 : hc : alk. paper)
    ISBN-13: 978-0-8160-6905-7 (v. 10 : hc : alk. paper)
    ISBN-10: 0-8160-6905-0 (v. 10 : hc : alk. paper)
    ISBN-13: 978-0-8160-6906-4 (v. 11 : hc : alk. paper)
    ISBN-10: 0-8160-6906-9 (v. 11 : hc : alk. paper)
    1. Vocational guidance—United States. 2. Occupations—United States. 3. Professions—United States.
    HF5382.5.U5T677 2007
    331.7020973—dc22

                                                                              2006028638

Contents

How to Use This Book

This book, part of the *Top Careers in Two Years* series, highlights in-demand careers for readers considering a two-year degree program—either straight out of high school or after working a job that does not require advanced education. The focus throughout is on the fastest-growing jobs with the best potential for advancement in the field. Readers learn about future prospects while discovering jobs they may never have heard of.

An associate's degree can be a powerful tool in launching a career. This book tells you how to use it to your advantage, explore job opportunities, and find local degree programs that meet your needs.

Each chapter provides the essential information needed to find not just a job but a career that fits your particular skills and interests. All chapters include the following features:

- **"Vital Statistics"** provides crucial information at a glance, such as salary range, employment prospects, education or training needed, and work environment.

- Discussion of salary and wages notes hourly versus salaried situations as well as potential benefits. Salary ranges take into account regional differences across the United States.

- **"Keys to Success"** is a checklist of personal skills and interests needed to thrive in the career.

- **"A Typical Day at Work"** describes what to expect at a typical day on the job.

- **"Two-Year Training"** lays out the value of an associate's degree for that career and what you can expect to learn.

- **"What to Look For in a School"** provides questions to ask and factors to keep in mind when selecting a two-year program.

- **"The Future"** discusses prospects for the career going forward.

- **"Interview with a Professional"** presents firsthand information from someone working in the field.

- ➤ "Job-Seeking Tips" offers suggestions on how to meet and work with people in the field, including how to get an internship or apprenticeship.

- ➤ "Career Connections" lists Web addresses of trade organizations providing more information about the career.

- ➤ "Associate's Degree Programs" provides a sampling of some of the better-known two-year schools.

- ➤ "Financial Aid" provides career-specific resources for financial aid.

- ➤ "Related Careers" lists similar related careers to consider.

In addition to a handy comprehensive index, the back of the book features two appendices providing invaluable information on job hunting and financial aid. Appendix A, Tools for Career Success, provides general tips on interviewing either for a job or two-year program, constructing a strong résumé, and gathering professional references. Appendix B, Financial Aid, introduces the process of applying for aid and includes information about potential sources of aid, who qualifies, how to prepare an application, and much more.

Introduction

Business makes the economy go round. Even the most primitive societies have their own forms of buying and selling, creating, growing, and sharing. Any time you bring more than two humans together, you will inevitably have business. Going into a business career is a sure bet to being a permanent part of the world's economy. Business is a world filled with opportunity, because there are as many kinds of businesses as there are products, services, and ideas.

One of the great things about a business career is that achievement is judged in dollars and cents, not credentials. If you work hard and take the initiative; if you bring in new business and make money; if you make customers happy and return for more, you will be headed for promotion. In the final analysis, it is whether you can do the job and do it well that makes the successful businessperson, not the diploma.

There are pros and cons to getting an associate's degree in order to go into business. These days, many who achieve high positions in corporate America have M.B.A.s (master's of business administration), not to mention bachelor degrees. On the other hand, one of the richest, most successful businesspeople in the world dropped out of college to work—Bill Gates of Microsoft fame.

For jobs that require less academic but more technical business skills, the right two-year degree can launch a highly successful career. Business skills such as word processing, spreadsheet and computer programs, stenography, filing and organizing, sales, teamwork, and human relations are taught in many associate's degree programs that lead straight to work. The careers outlined in this book capitalize on many of these skills.

For someone who doesn't want to devote four years to college, or can't afford it, a smart alternative is to get an associate's degree in business that can lead straight to work or can be a stepping-stone to a bachelor's later on—if you decide you need one. For millions of Americans, associate's degrees provide the essential training needed to pursue a rewarding career without the expense of a four-year degree. The U.S. Department of Education's National Center for Education Statistics estimates that by the end of 2005, more than 6.1 million students will have enrolled in degree-granting two-year institutions. The number of associate's degrees conferred continues to increase each year.

Compared with those who hold only a high school degree, associate's degree holders earn more money ($2,000–$6,000 a year more on average) and face a much lower rate of unemployment. Also, consider that 43 percent of four-year college grads are underemployed. On the other hand, there's a shortage of people with technical skills, including those trained at the two-year level.

"A four-year degree is a ticket to get in line for an oversold airplane," says Kenneth C. Gray, a professor of workforce education and development at Penn State University. For people with technical skills, however, including those trained at the two-year level, "There's more seats on the airplane than people holding tickets."

Flexibility is one of the main attractions of two-year degrees. Classes often are offered at night, close to home, or on the Internet. (However, don't be scammed—be sure to check out *accreditation* under "Finding the Right School.") Those looking for the more traditional college experience will find that about 20 percent of two-year colleges provide housing, cafeterias, sports, clubs, and a bustling social scene.

Another great feature of associate's degree programs is that admission is not overly competitive. Students are admitted from a wide range of academic backgrounds. Someone who performed below average in high school can excel at a two-year school if they put in the time and energy.

Also, because associate degree programs are very occupation-oriented, students spend a lot of their time getting "hands-on" experience. They either work on-site at actual businesses or they perform practical exercises in the classroom that give them real-world experience. For example, students in Alexandria Technical College's Finance and Credit Management program (see Chapter 5) finish with a paid internship at a financial institution. This real-world experience is often invaluable in landing an entry-level position. Many internships and apprenticeships lead directly to full-time employment.

Also, many people who start with a two-year degree continue on with their higher education—pursuing a four-year degree and often transferring credits earned from their two-year program. (When you investigate two-year programs, find out if your credits will be transferable or not before you sign the dotted line.) Some even go on to earn a more advanced professional degree. Often, if you pursue academics directly related to your job, your employer will pay some or all of your tuition.

An Affordable Route

The latest statistics from the College Board show that the average total for annual tuition and fees for 2005–2006 at a four-year private college is $21,235, while the annual cost at a public two-year institution averages $2,191. And financial aid is not just for four-year college students—those attending trade, technical, vocational, two-year, and career colleges can also qualify for aid. The College Board reports that grant aid averages about $2,300 per student for those attending two-year public colleges. Schools that offer federal financing must be accredited though, and the U.S. Department of Education provides a list of accredited institutions at http://www.ope.ed.gov/accreditation/index.asp.

Just as with four-year students, two-year students who want a piece of the aid pie usually must file the Free Application for Federal Student Aid (FAFSA). Lenders are increasingly helping the two-year student as well. SallieMae (http://www.salliemae.com), the federal student loan agency, offers very specific private loans for career training, and U.S. Bank just introduced the CampUS Education Loan specifically for those attending two-year schools. (For more information on financial aid, see Appendix B.)

Loans and Scholarships

As you decide how to finance your associate's degree for a career in business, it helps to know a few basic facts about financial aid. For instance, scholarships and grants are financial awards that do not have to be paid back; a loan must be paid back with interest. Make sure you understand the terms of the loan (when you will begin to pay and how much interest you will pay) before you agree to it.

Business students can try a search for financial aid at http://www.businessschools.com/financial-aid/. Also check out the U.S. Department of Education at http://www.ed.gov/finaid/info/find/edpicks.jhtml?src=ov. Often the school you apply to will help with financial aid resources and even scholarships. You can search online for scholarships at http://www.fastweb.com/. This Web site pops up commercial offers, especially from colleges. If you do not wish to be contacted, keep clicking on "No thanks." Once you get through the lengthy questionnaire, you will get a good list of possible scholarships.

Most importantly, make sure that you do not fall prey to scholarship scams. You should not have to pay money in order to apply for a scholarship or a loan. Legitimate scholarship grantors do not ask you for money. To check out more about scholarship scams, go to http://www.finaid.org/scholarships/scams.phtml.

Stepping-stones

An associate's degree can be a stepping-stone to the workplace as well as to further education. This is particularly true for a career in business. Business is a realm of opportunities; you may end up doing a job you never even imagined. After working for a while, you may decide that going back to school for a B.A. or an M.B.A. would be a great career move. To have that flexibility later on, you should understand your options before you even begin your two-year college program.

Most two-year colleges offer an associate in science (A.S.), an associate in applied science (A.A.S.), an associate in arts (A.A.), and certificate programs. The associate in arts focuses on studies in humanities and social sciences; certificate programs (usually one-year programs) help certify the student to do a certain job such as paramedic, database manager, or sign language interpreter.

The business student usually pursues either an associate in science or an associate in applied science. The "applied" part of the A.A.S. degree indicates that the program is specifically geared for students who want to go straight to work, applying the skills learned. The associate in science (A.S.) is geared for students who wish to transfer directly into a four-year bachelor's program at another school.

To be a savvy business student, you should ask prospective colleges about these degrees and what your options will be after you graduate. If you complete the A.A.S. degree in business, how much of your course work will apply toward a bachelor of arts (B.A.) or a bachelor of science (B.S.) if you eventually decide to return to school? If you choose an A.S. in business instead of the A.A.S., will you learn the skills you need to go to straight to work in your chosen field? And if the school offers a certificate program that interests you, can you combine that program with an A.A.S. or an A.S. in Business?

Both the A.S. and the A.A.S. in business are useful degrees; you should decide on the basis of your goals which two-year degree will be best for you.

Finding the Right School

Two-year colleges abound, and there may be one close to home. Even so, don't dive into the closest college program without doing some research first. It is important to review different schools to understand what your local college may and may not offer. There might be another local school better suited to your interests. Or you might decide to go away to school and live with relatives, with a friend, or in a dormitory.

A good place to begin your search for the right two-year college is online at http://www.collegeboard.com You can create a profile of exactly what kind of school and program you want, in whatever location you want, and see which colleges come up. Another good place to begin your search is in the library; most libraries carry college directories and many individual catalogues. Be sure to investigate each college that looks interesting with a search of the college's Web site; review their catalog; and you may even call the college's admissions office and arrange to have a chat with someone at the school.

Whatever college you choose, make sure that it is accredited by one of the agencies recognized by the United States Department of Education. Be aware that some "colleges" may appear legitimate but might not be accredited or recognized by the U.S. Department of Education. Don't go through all that hard work and end up with a nonaccredited degree! You can check "Diploma Mills and Accreditation" at the U.S. Department of Education's Web site (http://www.ed.gov/students/prep/college/diplomamills/index.html). More information is available at the Council for Higher Education Accreditation (http://www.chea.org).

Regional and National Accrediting Agencies Recognized by the United States Department of Education

* Accrediting Council for Independent Colleges and Schools
* Distance Education and Training Council
* Middle States Association of Colleges and Schools
* New England Association of Schools and Colleges
* North Central Association of Colleges and Schools
* Northwest Association of Schools and Colleges
* Southern Association of Colleges and Schools
* Western Association of Schools and Colleges

The Entrepreneur

One exciting kind of business is as basic as the American dream—going into business for yourself. Entrepreneurship is not a chapter in this book because it is not advisable to begin your business career as an independent business owner. Most new businesses do not make a profit for the first one to three years. Even more important, for the business beginner, there is too much to learn and too many mistakes to be made. It is better to learn, to make mistakes, and to be guided by a more experienced mentor while working for someone else. You will learn more while making a regular salary!

Anyone who has a skill or service to offer and who understands business can go into business for him- or herself. For example, you might be a freelance court reporter, an independent insurance adjuster, or a fitness trainer. Like freelance court reporter Joanne Mincy (Chapter 6), you might work for an agency that provides jobs for you. If you have big ambitions, you could eventually open an agency yourself. Many insurance adjusters like Jared Stuart (Chapter 3) work for independent adjusting agencies, companies that represent the client (not the insurance company). After working in the field and learning the ropes, some adjusters go on to open their own independent businesses. Fitness trainer Justin Schulman (Chapter 10) plunged right into his own business soon after he got started in the field. People in the trades (such as auto mechanics, electricians, plumbers, chefs) often go on to open their own small businesses. Anyone with a skill or service that is in demand, business know-how, a desire for independence, a big dose of self-discipline, plus plenty of ambition, can become an entrepreneur. American business history is full of confident, adventurous men and women who had a great idea and made their fortunes going into business for themselves.

Finding the Right Business Job

Whether your ultimate goal is to work for yourself or not, you'll probably want the security of working for someone else initially. So here are a few tips about finding the right business job once you have completed your business associate's degree and are ready for the workplace.

For office support jobs (office manager, executive secretary, human resources assistant), look for work in an industry you like. That may be fashion, publishing, advertising, public service, video production, or whatever catches your imagination. Once you begin to work in an industry, you will learn a lot about it, and you might go on to other jobs within the company.

When you interview for a job, dress for success. For business, that means "conservative." Wear a suit and very low profile jewelry. Even for a business where everyone dresses casually, an interview demands your best clothes and good grooming. If you make a poor first impression, you will probably lose the job right then and there. And don't forget that you are interviewing the company too. Do you like their style? Are these people you will be comfortable with? In what space would you actually work? Do you like the job description? What about benefits, such as health insurance or sick leave? (Note: Don't ask about benefits until the end of the interview. If you ask too soon, it makes you sound more interested in the perks than the job.) For additional job-hunting tips, turn to Appendix A.

Once you begin a job, always be ready to give 150 percent! Do more than is expected of you. Take the initiative. Ask how you can help. Hard work is always noticed and rewarded. If you are interested in advancement in the company, learn everything you can about your company and the business itself. You can tell your boss about your ambitions, but don't do it right away. Show your talent, initiative, and hard work before you talk about wanting to take on more responsibility or move on to a bigger job.

Sometimes the best way to advance your career is to change companies. Stay in one job for two to five years, then brush up your résumé and look for more money and more responsibility somewhere else. Working for a few different businesses can give you a broader perspective on your job and, if you lose your position for any reason, it can make you better equipped to find a new job. On the other hand, a résumé that shows a job change every year spells trouble; the lack of commitment will raise red flags for recruiters. Move on only after you have learned everything you can from the job you have, and you're on your way to establishing a successful business career!

Office Manager

> ## Vital Statistics
>
> **Salary:** Salaries for office managers range from $25,190 or less to more than $67,800 a year; the median yearly salary is $41,030 according to 2006 figures from the U.S. Bureau of Labor Statistics.
>
> **Employment:** Due to emerging technology and decreasing need for support staff, the field of office management will be more competitive, with growth somewhat slower than the average for all occupations through 2014, according to the bureau. However, this position will remain indispensable for all businesses both large and small.
>
> **Education:** Business school certificate or an associate's degree in business administration/management or administrative/secretarial services is advisable. Office experience is a must.
>
> **Work Environment:** Offices in small to large firms and organizations. Usually office managers work in a clean, comfortable, and well-organized environment.

Think of a really good juggler who is smiling and joking while keeping ten balls in the air at once and you've got the image of a great office manager. The office manager is responsible for many different jobs that are vital to running a business; what you do today may be entirely different from what you'll need to do tomorrow. Most of all, an office manager helps the company's workflow proceed smoothly without interruption.

Although some of your responsibilities will depend upon the size and kind of business you work for, some tasks are typical. You will interview and hire staff, supervise others, maintain office equipment, and order supplies *before* they run out. You may do specific accounting jobs, or you may supervise these jobs. Filing and organizing the company's records will be in your hands, and good computer skills are critical. Overall, organization is key. You must anticipate the needs of the company and make sure that everyone is able to do his or her job efficiently.

As an office manager, you might work in almost any business imaginable. Jobs run the gamut from advertising to zoo management. You might work for a hospital, publisher, sports and fitness center, software company, school, or physician's office. If the business employs more than four or five people, chances are the front office will need a manager.

Many people who achieve the position of office manager are promoted from within a company. It is helpful to understand the needs of your specific organization in order to run the office effectively. In addition, companies typically hire someone for this job who has several years of office experience. A good place to begin a career as an office manager is by working as an administrative assistant or other support staff. If you shine in this position by always going the extra mile, by taking the initiative to do more than is required, chances are you will be noticed as a person with good management potential.

The good news about this career is that effective office management is vital to a successful business. The bad new is that computer programs and other technologies enable more executives, managers, and specialists to manage their own needs. However, though there may be fewer staff to manage, the demand for office managers will remain strong. Both small and large businesses will always need someone to manage these essential services. In 2004, over 1.5 million people held jobs as office managers or administrative supervisors.

Opportunities in office management can arise when office managers are promoted. If you are ready, you may be promoted too. And because this career offers opportunity to advance, you should think carefully about the kind of business to target in your career search. Is this an industry that excites you, something that you would like to learn more about? Can you see yourself rising in management or furthering your education to learn more specific skills? If so, it will be worth beginning on the ground floor and working your way up.

On the Job

No matter what kind of business they work for, office managers must be one thing: responsible. People can count on them to get things done. They ensure that others always have the supplies they need; they also may be the one who says "no" when someone wants something that is too extravagant.

People call the office manager when something goes wrong and when things go right. For instance, an office manager not only must find the repairperson to fix the lights, he or she also plans the parties and hires the caterers. An office manager might do the company's bookkeeping, banking, and bills, or supervise the bookkeeper. He or she might oversee office renovations, buy office furniture, hire a new receptionist, teach that new hire how to operate the phones and photocopy machine, and fix the photocopy machine when the paper gets stuck. The office managers' job is to smooth the way for other members of the company to do their best.

Some office managers say "being firm" is their most important asset. As a supervisor and organizer, an office manager must be able to establish consistent guidelines and ensure the staff follows them. They must evaluate the performance of others and dismiss ineffective staff. At the same time, they may need to help someone who is having problems or to resolve office disputes. An office manager is a motivator and teacher, as well as a supervisor.

Specialized offices, such as medical or dental offices, may require special skills. For example, the medical office manager needs to understand health insurance and reimbursements. If this field interests you, look for schools that offer programs especially geared to medical office management.

Office experience is an essential requirement for an office management job. Important office experience can be gained by working part time while still in school, or by taking an internship. Office managers are often promoted from within the company, so it can be a good career move to begin with a different administrative job and work toward promotion to office manager.

> ## "The key to being a good manager is keeping the people who hate me away from those who are still undecided."
> —Casey Stengel, former Yankees manager

 ## Keys to Success

To be a successful office manager, you should have strong

- organizational ability
- attention to detail
- communication skills
- computer skills
- decision-making skills
- leadership skills

Do You Have What It Takes?

Take a look around your bedroom and study area. Are these areas neat and well organized? Anyone who aspires to the position of office manager should have a knack for organization. If you like turning chaos into structure, you may have what it takes. You also enjoy working on a team and helping others succeed. Communication skills are essential. You should like English classes, find good grammar easy, and enjoy writing and public speaking. In addition to studying high school math and technology, make sure you are fast and accurate on a keyboard; proficiency with Microsoft Office Suite is recommended.

A Typical Day at Work

You unlock the door, walk into the office, and already, the phone is ringing. The receptionist is late again, and a vice president is stuck in traffic, worried about an early appointment. You find the VP's files and set up a comfortable spot with coffee for the client to wait until the VP gets in. Meanwhile, the CFO (chief financial officer) arrives and meets with you about the new bookkeeping software you have recommended.

Before lunch, you meet with the receptionist and discuss his lateness problem. You advise a new alarm clock and let him know he will be dismissed if he is late again. You order lunch and conduct a lunchtime training session with four secretaries. You are teaching them PowerPoint, a presentation software program that is part of the Microsoft Office Suite.

The afternoon begins with a crisis: The bank did not receive the lawyer's notarized papers. You make phone calls, find out the papers are in the bank's mailroom, and get them delivered to the right person. You distribute the new ergonomic mouse pads, check supplies, and sit down at your desk to attack your paperwork. Later, you circulate, saying hello and seeing if anybody needs anything. Suddenly, there's another crisis—a plugged-up sink in the office kitchen. You get the superintendent to fix it, check a clerk's progress on inventory control, remind your receptionist to be on time, and set up for your busy day tomorrow.

How to Break In

First, find a business or industry that interests and excites you. Are there any special skills or knowledge that would make you especially useful in that industry? If so, add them to your list of office skills to learn as you prepare for your career. While still in school, work part time as an administrative assistant or clerk, and add a summer internship if you can. In these jobs, make sure you shine. Always do more than is expected. Volunteer for extra responsibility whenever you can. Ask for the opportunity to help or supervise someone new. Once you have solid administrative experience and you have demonstrated an ability to supervise, you will be a good candidate for the office management job. If the job does not open up in your office, you might look for an office management job with another company in the same industry. Be sure to ask for a letter of recommendation from your supervisor before you leave.

Two-Year Training

A college degree is not a prerequisite to become an office manager, but it helps. Most community colleges offer an associate's degree in business that will prepare you well for office management. Your major might be business management, business administration, or administrative services.

Before deciding what area of business to major in, talk to the school's career-development office. Your specific major will depend upon the industry you hope to work in, the areas of business you like, and the skills you need to develop.

Whatever your major, it will be wise to include courses in finance such as accounting and bookkeeping. Because you will need to manage people, to understand their problems and resolve their conflicts, you also should study psychology, organizational behavior, and sociology. And because communication—both spoken and written—will be important on the job, you should study English and writing.

Specific technical skills are important, too. It is essential to have good computer skills, including proficiency in software programs for word processing, spreadsheets, and finance. Employers often look for proficiency in Microsoft Office Suite.

Some additional skills are needed to become an office manager for the two highest-paying jobs: the medical office and the law office. Doctor, dentist, and hospital offices require an understanding of medical terminology and complex insurance forms. A law office expects its office managers to have backgrounds as paralegals or legal secretaries.

A medical office may hire clerical staff without medical-office training, but specialized training will put you ahead of the game. The Professional Association of Health Care Office Management (http://www.pahcom.com) offers a certificate program. Law offices can be even more demanding in terms of qualifications. If law office management is your goal, your best bet is to get special training as a legal secretary or paralegal. Add some business-management training as well as law-office experience, and you will be an ideal candidate.

What to Look For in a School

While most community colleges and many technical schools offer certificates or associate's degree programs in business, you can narrow your choices by asking these questions:

☞ Will the school teach me how to use the necessary software programs?

☞ Does the school teach business writing? What about organizational and management skills?

☞ What kind of support is available outside of class if I find myself having trouble learning the skills I need?

☞ Have the professors worked in business themselves, especially as managers?

☞ Does the school help students find summer internships?

☞ Does the school have a good job-placement program? What is the school's job-placement rate?

☞ Will this school prepare me to get a job in the industry I want?

Interview with a Professional:
Q&A
Kathleen Pryor

Office manager, Partners in Brainstorms, Inc.,
Phoenix, Arizona

Q: *How did you get started?*

A: I was hired at Partners in Brainstorms Inc. as a youth event coordinator; then I was asked to update computer systems and software. Today, I do everything from setting up office security, ordering services, helping with accounting, and reviewing health-insurance policies to organizing the company calendar, joining network associations to increase business opportunities, and working closely with current clients and the president of the company.

Q: *What's a typical day like?*

A: Working for a small company, my responsibilities change with each project. Every morning I have my "To Do List," but I have to be flexible for the unexpected. When a situation arises that needs immediate attention, I have to be quick to solve the problem. Through experience on the job, I've learned who to contact, where to go, what to do, and how to solve the problem. To make problem-solving stress free, it helps to have my resources at my fingertips. It's extremely important to be organized. Every day my goal is to accomplish tasks, to get the job done, and to have a productive day.

Q: *What is your advice for those starting a career?*

A: You have to have excellent communication and organizational skills. Be responsible and take your job seriously. People depend on you to get the job done and get it right the first time. Also, if something goes wrong, do your best to solve the situation and don't take it personally. Be professional and people will recognize your hard work.

Q: *What is the best part of being an office manager?*

A: What I love most is when I go on vacation, and my staff realizes how important I am to helping the office run smoothly.

The Future

While it is predicted that office management will be a slower-than-average growth field because of automation, good managers will still be in demand. The entry-level position of clerk or administrative assistant is one of the easiest first jobs to get, and successful administrative assistants often advance to become office managers. However, the competition will be keen. Prepare yourself well. If you have the skills, experience, and dedication, all you will need is the opportunity. It is worth noting that the same skills that equip you to be an office manager are also very much in demand for secretaries and executive assistants.

Whether a job in office management is your main goal or a stepping-stone, once you have proven yourself, you may become a candidate to move up the corporate ladder. At that time, you might decide to go back to school for your bachelor's degree, or go on to a master's in business administration. Or you might find the time is right to get more specific training in the industry for which you work.

Did You Know?

One of 2006's top shows, "The Office" revolves around the life of an office manager, played by comedian Steve Carrell.

Job Seeking Tips

Follow these specific tips for office managers and turn to Appendix A for help on résumés and interviewing.

✔ To get experience, work in an office as an intern, summer or part-time hire, or as a volunteer.

✔ After you intern or when you leave a part-time job, ask for a letter of recommendation from your office supervisor.

✔ Practice keyboarding to build speed and accuracy. You probably will be tested!

✔ Explore various industries and search for a job in an industry you like.

✔ Be sure to dress for success. An office manager should appear to be neat, organized, and professional.

Career Connections

For further information, contact the following organizations.

The **Association of Professional Office Managers**. This comprehensive site includes information on training, conferences, new software, and an online magazine.   http://www.apomhq.org

The **International Association of Administrative Professionals**. This site offers news and information for all administrative professionals. http://www.iaap-hq.org

The **National Association of Legal Secretaries, Inc.** http://www.nals.org

The **Professional Association of Health Care Office Management** http://www.pahom.com

National Management Association http://www.nma1.org

Associate's Degree Programs

Many colleges offer associate's degrees in business. Here are a few:

Henry Ford Community College, Dearborn, Michigan

Jefferson State Community College, Birmingham, Alabama

Everest College, Phoenix, Arizona; Dallas, Texas; and other cities

CUNY: Borough of Manhattan Community College, New York, New York

Illinois Central College, East Peoria, Illinois

Financial Aid

Some businesses will pay for an employee's tuition if the college program enhances the employee's on-the-job skills. Be sure to turn to Appendix B for more information.

Financial Aid for Business Students lists many financial aid resources. http://www.businessschools.com/financial-aid/

Related Careers

Bookkeeper, facilities manager, paralegal, and court reporter.

Accounts Payable Administrator

Salary: Depending on duties, job location, and other factors, pay can be less than $20,000 a year or more than $40,000; the median for accounts payable workers is $28,570, according to the 2006 data from the U.S. Bureau of Labor Statistics.

Employment: Accounts payable workers are as valuable as ever, but the growth of new jobs will be slow due to accounting software innovations, downsizing, and outsourcing to other countries.

Education: Accounts payable does not require a college degree, but to advance to a management position, an associate's degree in business is advisable.

Work Environment: An accounts payable administrator is a desk jockey, logging in heavy computer time and working with papers and files in an orderly, clean, well-lit office environment for a large or small company, or the government.

What if someone you didn't know very well could sign and hand out checks from your family's bank account? And that person was in charge of paying your family's debts, such as credit card bills, gas and electric bills, and your very own cell phone bill? Would you want that person to have a supervisor?

It's a good bet your answer is yes. In business, this kind of supervisor or manager is called the accounts payable administrator. The accounts payable administrator is the person who keeps tabs on where the money is, and watches who is getting paid for what.

When businesses need supplies, materials, or services, they buy from vendors. A business needs everything a family does, and more—health insurance, electricity, telephones, plus special equipment or raw materials that may be used in the business. After you purchase something, the vendor bills your business and expects to be paid in a timely manner. The accounts payable department pays the bills.

If it sounds simple, be warned: It isn't. When using a company's money, there must be a rigorous paper trail. To purchase anything requires a *purchase order* form. Purchases, vendors, and payments must be logged (kept track of). If vendors have standing orders, *invoices* (the vendor's bill to your company) and payments may overlap. Invoices and payments must be matched to the purchase orders and checked for accuracy. Computerized records must also match the paper inventories, and balances must tally up correctly at the end of the month or the quarter (a three-month period).

Attention to all this detail is important to maintain the company's financial health. By keeping management informed about expenditures and balances in various accounting ledgers, the accounts payable administrator can help management maintain a financially sound business.

Just as important is the accounts payable administrator's responsibility to prevent fraud and theft. Occasionally, through a variety of deceptive practices, accounts payable personnel may try to pay themselves or others what they have not earned. Most companies have internal controls to prevent this kind of embezzlement. Usually two signatures are required on any check. Often the clerk who writes out the check is not the person who reviews and signs it. The accounts payable administrator is the one who makes sure it all adds up the way it should at the end of the month.

On the Job

While many accounts payable employees work a regular 40-hour week and keep typical business hours, this is a field where skilled, part-time workers are valued as well. In certain industries that have busy and slow seasons, such as retail stores and hotels, certain times of the year may require overtime work. Some bookkeepers and accounting personnel work in the evenings or on weekends, especially at "crunch" times such as tax time or before a monthly audit.

Because there is so much desk and computer work, accounts payable administrators may experience eye and muscle strain, backaches, or headaches. It is important to be vigilant about taking exercise breaks and to adjust office equipment properly to prevent repetitive motion injuries.

As an accounts payable supervisor, you will have a variety of responsibilities. In addition to overseeing clerks and other personnel, the supervisor is entrusted to make sure the department functions smoothly. You may be asked to oversee payroll and expense account vouchers, and you will be expected to prepare appropriate accounting reports. Because your function will involve interacting with subordinate personnel, upper management, and vendors, good communication skills will be an important asset.

Keys to Success

To be a successful accounts payable administrator, you should have strong

- math skills
- organizational skills
- trustworthiness
- attention to detail
- spreadsheet and financial software experience
- bookkeeping and accounting skills

Do You Have What It Takes?

To make it in accounts payable, you should have a passion for numbers, order, and precision. You must be able to catch errors where others overlook them. Your work will be meticulous. Gossip has no place in the accounts payable office; you will come into contact with confidential material, and discretion and trustworthiness are essential. What's more, you must be scrupulously honest.

> ### "The best indicator of a sound company is one that pays its bills in a timely manner."
> — *Beginner's Guide to Accounting*

A Typical Day at Work

You love your job as accounts payable supervisor at a large magazine publishing company, but today something seems off. As you review a major vendor's account, you suddenly get alarmed. Is someone at this vendor actually stealing payments?

It looks as though the vendor has invoiced you repeatedly for the same printing bill! You start working back through the records of purchase orders, invoices, and payments. You assign two clerks to double check the computer printouts against the original file of purchase orders going back for almost one year.

Meanwhile, you have to get a second signature for payroll checks and help a new clerk verify some expense-account receipts and petty-cash vouchers. In the afternoon, you work on a new, inter-departmental expense reporting system. Once it's up, data gathering will be more efficient, and you will be able to improve the quarterly report. Just after you take a break for a walk around the block, your two clerks inform you that the total owed to the printing vendor is correct. The vendor applied a check sent for invoice #373 to invoice #371 and #372, thus making it look like they were double-billing. You authorize payment and end your day in a meeting with the company comptroller and the director of marketing for a company magazine. You advise them against starting a new marketing campaign until the current series of radio ads has been paid. Five o'clock rolls around faster than you would have thought possible.

How to Break In

While someone outside the company with great credentials might be hired as a supervisor in accounts payable, most companies are likely to promote from within. Start in an industry you like as an accounts-payable or book-keeping clerk. Make sure you have the keyboard and software skills that will make you valuable to the company. Some companies will offer further training or initial on-the-job training from a senior worker. Advance within the company by taking on more work, or more complicated work (hopefully for more pay). If your goal is to be a supervisor or manager, let your manager know that you would like to help others or take on more responsibility. If you think it might help, you can also further your career with on-line courses.

Two-Year Training

Most community colleges and business schools offer a two-year associate's degree in business. Most likely, you will want to major in accounting or accounting technology; there is no specific major for accounts payable. Inquire at the school what courses would be best for a career in accounts payable. Your courses should definitely include bookkeeping and several accounting classes, such as cost accounting and managerial accounting. You may also take a class in tax concepts and statistics. Financial software training, including spreadsheets, is a must! Don't worry too much about the specific software program; as long as you have the basic skills, your on-the-job training can show you the details of other programs. You will also want to study business communications and get some management training under your belt. If you can, volunteer to clerk for free in the accounts payable department of a business near you. Even a few months of such work will pay off later when you interview for jobs.

What to Look For in a School

Ask these questions when you consider schools:

☞ Will this school train me in bookkeeping and accounting software?

☞ Do any teachers have experience in accounts payable?

☞ Can I combine accounting with management training? Can I learn a wide range of skills?

☞ Does this school offer any internship opportunities?

☞ What is the school's job placement rate?

Interview with a Professional: Q&A

Susan Tinkler-Muller

Director—accounting services, MTV Networks,
New York, New York

Q: *How did you get started in accounts payable?*

A: I was commuting, via train, to my job at the time—in insurance—and I met a woman who worked for MTV. She frequently talked to me about the department she ran, and I was always interested. She told me about a job opportunity for an entry-level position, and after a few interviews I was offered the job as a check clerk. It was my job to "match" the checks, obtain check signatures and deliver the checks internally. Since then I have held many positions within accounts payable and have been managing the department since 1997.

Q: *What is a typical day like as an accounts payable manager?*

A: I'd have to say that there is no typical day in accounts payable, especially in the entertainment industry. Sure, there's data entry, check cutting, and mailing, but that's only part of what an accounts payable department does. There are so many other cool job functions: petty cash, auditor, banking, systems, and reporting and reconciliations, just to name a few.

Q: *What is your advice for those starting a career in accounts payable?*

A: Regardless of the tasks performed, do your best. It's through hard work and self-education that I have been able to achieve my current position.

Q: *What is the best part of being an accounts payable manager?*

A: I like the satisfaction I get with this job. I enjoy working with people, and accounts payable allows you to work with both internal and external customers. In addition, I feel as though I have learned many other job functions just by managing accounts payable.

The Future

The sheer size of this occupation, especially in the entry-level position, ensures many job openings. Bookkeeping, accounting, and auditing clerks held more than 2 million jobs in 2006. Of these, about 25 percent worked part time. These jobs are available in all industries and branches of government. However, due to office automation, slow growth is projected for accounts payable positions. In addition, many of the lower-level jobs continue to be outsourced to other countries where workers are paid less. The wider the range of financial and management abilities you have, the more you will be in demand.

Did You Know?

In a 2006 survey, the Enterprise Strategy Group found that confidential data was the most vulnerable to insider attacks from employees, contractors, and outsourcing partners.

Job Seeking Tips

Follow these specific tips for accounts payable administrator and turn to Appendix A for help on résumés and interviewing.

✔ Seek an entry-level job in an industry you like or an area of government you find interesting, then work your way up to an a dministrator's position.

✔ Read some articles from the accounts payable Web sites below. They may offer ideas for your job search and for interview discussions.

✔ Present a tidy and conservative appearance on your interview. Look as organized as your accounts payable department will be.

✔ Be prepared to discuss your software training and your knowledge of bookkeeping. Make sure you know the jargon.

✔ Ask yourself how would you respond to the interview question: "How can I be sure you are trustworthy?"

Career Connections

For further information, look up the following organizations at these Web sites.

International Accounts Payable Professionals http://www.iappnet.org (non-profit educational)

The AP Network http://www.theapnetwork.com (for-profit association by membership, a seven-day free trial offer is available)

Associate's Degree Programs

Many colleges offer associate's degrees in business with a specialty in accounting. Here are a few:

City College of San Francisco, San Francisco, California

AIB College of Business, Des Moines, Iowa

Forsyth Technical Community College, Winston-Salem, North Carolina

Miami Dade College, Miami, Florida

Community College of Philadelphia, Philadelphia, Pennsylvania

Financial Aid

Scholarships for students majoring in accounting abound. Minority associations are especially interested in encouraging students in this area. On the downside, many of the scholarships are for bachelor's degree candidates; some, however, only require enrollment in a degree program. Check out these sites, and see if you find a scholarship that fits your needs. Also investigate your state's CPA society for financial aid. Turn to Appendix B for more information on financial aid for two-year students.

The **American Institute of Certified Public Accountants.** For a variety of scholarship information, search on "scholarships" at http://www.aicpa.org or check out http://www.aicpa.org/nolimits/ become/ships/AICPA.htm. This Web site may include more scholarships for four-year programs than two-year programs.

The **Association of Latino Professionals in Finance and Accounting** offers scholarships to Latino students who are enrolled in a college program in the area of financial services or accounting.   http://www .alpfa.org

The **National Association of Black Accountants, Inc.** offers scholarships to African-American college students getting a degree in accounting.   http://www.nabainc.org/pages/Student_ScholarshipProgram.jsp

The **National Society of Accountants** has scholarships available for students who are associate's degree candidates in accounting. http://www.nsacct.org/foundation.asp

Related Careers

Bookkeeping, accounting, and auditing clerks work with financial records. Other clerks who perform similar duties include brokerage clerks, credit authorizers, payroll clerks, and bank tellers.

Insurance Adjuster

Vital Statistics

Salary: Insurance claims adjusters can earn from a low of $27,220 to a high of more than $72,620. The median is about $44,220, according to the 2006 figures from the U.S. Bureau of Labor Statistics.

Employment: There will be a continued need for insurance adjusters; job growth should be average.

Education: An associate's degree in business or an insurance specialty is advisable. Further training is sometimes available within an insurance company. Some states require licensing.

Work Environment: Insurance adjusters work in both the office and the field, with a variety of locations.

In the not-too-distant past, if a fire destroyed a family's house and the family had no money to rebuild, the family remained homeless or they scrambled for whatever inadequate housing they could get. If someone suffered an injury and needed treatment, he got treatment only if he could afford it. If a driver accidentally crashed into another car, destroying property and causing injury, he might lose his home and everything he owned in order to pay for the damages.

Today, insurance helps us avoid these kinds of financial disasters. Insurance adjusters, along with examiners, appraisers, and investigators, help process insurance claims. In general, an adjuster works on property and casualty (accident) insurance. Usually, an examiner works on life and health insurance.

Just like a lawyer, an insurance claims adjuster can work "either side of the street." This means the adjuster can work as an advocate for the individual who is making an insurance claim or for the insurance company that has to pay for the damage.

When the insurance adjuster works for an insurance company, the adjuster investigates insurance claims, negotiates settlements, and authorizes payments, based on guidelines provided by his or her employer. An insurance investigator may help the adjuster make sure no fraud is involved; an appraiser may help determine the worth of what was lost.

When the adjuster works for the person filing the insurance claim (the claimant), the adjuster does many of the same jobs. However, the adjuster's focus is on making sure that the claimant gets a fair settlement instead of making sure the insurance company is not defrauded. Called "public adjusters," insurance adjusters who advocate for claimants gener-ally work for an independent adjusters' company, though a few may go into business for themselves.

These days, new technologies help the insurance adjuster work more ef-fectively. The laptop computer, digital camera, and cell phone are all part of the modern adjuster's arsenal. Because the adjuster is the insurance com-pany's first line of defense against fraud, he or she regularly goes into the field to photograph evidence, interview claimants, and dispatch informa-tion to the company office via the Internet. The laptop also enables the ad-juster to download needed forms or access important information without delay. For some adjusters, having a laptop computer, cell phone, and com-pany car provided are "perks" of the job.

On the Job

Insurance adjusters generate and manage the flow of work needed to process claims. After receiving a claim, an insurance adjuster will begin the process by traveling to the site and assessing what is needed. The adjuster may consult with police, review hospital records, inspect property damage, photograph and document evidence, interview claimants and witnesses, and often will audio- or videotape interviews. If specialized expert infor-mation is needed, the adjuster may consult other professionals such as lawyers, architects, construction contractors, engineers, or accountants. If the job is very large or complex, a claims examiner may help the adjuster with these tasks.

When the claim is legitimate, the adjuster will work out a settlement with the claimant. However, when an insurance adjuster suspects fraud—such as a staged accident, a fake workers' disability, an unnecessary med-ical treatment, or a crime such as arson—the adjuster brings in an investigator, often a former law enforcement officer. As such a case pro-gresses, the insurance adjuster may be called upon to testify or to help the company expose the fraud.

On the other hand, the *public* adjuster will help the claimant get a fair deal. Working along the same lines as the insurance adjuster, the public ad-juster will collect evidence and interview experts. The public adjuster's job is to ensure that the claimant gets a fair and appropriate settlement and that his or her rights are respected.

A constantly changing scene sets the stage for the adjuster's job. Some adjusters spend little time in the office and are constantly traveling to claim sites such as the scene of a fire, the wreckage of a car, or the ruins left by a storm. The adjuster might travel to the home of a claimant's witness, a hos-pital room, or an expert's office.

Working hours can be irregular, including evenings or weekends. If there are many claims to investigate, the adjuster may be expected to work overtime. If there is a major emergency, such as a tornado or hurricane, the adjusters may need to leave home for days to travel to the disaster site and work with local adjusters. As the adjuster acquires experience, he or she may be able to telecommute, working from home and keeping in touch with the office by telephone and the Internet.

Keys to Success

To be a successful claims adjuster, you should have

- problem-solving, deductive-reasoning, and decision-making skills
- confidence and determination
- negotiation and communication skills
- basic computer skills
- self-motivation
- mathematical skills

Do You Have What It Takes?

If you prefer routine and stress-free days, this job is not for you. The successful insurance adjuster works under pressure from all sides and enjoys the challenge. Not only is this job similar to assembling a jigsaw puzzle in record time, an adjuster must find the pieces of the puzzle before he or she can even begin.

Each new claim is a new challenge to be solved. The adjuster will need to dig out the facts, evaluate them, and determine what kind of financial settlement is fair. When rushed, adjusters must be determined and thorough under pressure. When disputed, they must be confident in their judgments yet flexible enough to negotiate.

Other specific skills can be a plus on the job. Speaking another language can be very useful. Skills in auto mechanics, finance, and construction are in demand also for certain claims adjuster positions.

How to Break In

With the right training, experience, and skills, you can start a great career as an insurance adjuster. The first step is to check out the licensing requirements for an insurance adjuster in your state. Some states require very little, and others ask for specific training plus a licensing test. Sometimes it is possible for an adjuster to work under the license of the insurance company. For specific requirements, check out your state's department of insurance.

While a degree in insurance is not necessary, a two-year degree is helpful. It will be especially helpful to complete an internship at an insurance agency. Many insurance agencies have internship programs; visit the Web site of any large agency near you to find internship opportunities.

Because adjusters work in all kinds of industries from health care to engineering, experience or basic coursework in a variety of areas can be an asset to getting a job as an insurance adjuster. These include business, accounting, engineering, health care, automotive technology, or law.

Sometimes adjusters move into their jobs after they become familiar with the insurance industry through entry-level jobs. Entry-level jobs in insurance include sales, administrative work, or customer service in the claims department. Some companies will pay for further insurance education or college coursework.

A Typical Day at Work

After checking in at the office, you find you have five new claims to investigate. You take your company car to the site of a fire where you meet the homeowners. Sitting on their porch, you take down the information on your company laptop, entering the data on the claims software system and making a few extra notes to yourself on a pad of paper. Once you have taken pictures of the damage, you get the facts from the police and fire department on the phone and make more entries on your laptop.

Back at the office, you make more detailed notes about your talk with the house's owners. The notes might be used in court some day, so you are careful to remember every detail. A different homeowner whose basement was damaged by a broken pipe calls you to complain that he still can't fix his pipes because you haven't given him an answer yet. After calming the homeowner, you make some more calls to try to speed up the man's claim.

Another visit that afternoon takes you to an automotive repair shop, where you are told that the damage is inconsistent with the claim. You suspect that the owner's teenage son, who was not covered under the insurance, might have been driving. Back at the office again, you call a company investigator and ask her to look into the claim a little further. You also make calls to set up appointments to begin the investigations of your other new claims. Next, you get a call from your manager questioning the payment you okayed for a gas-heater explosion.

Your day ends with a meeting to negotiate a settlement for another homeowner who needs a roof repair after a tree fell on the house. You meet the clients' lawyer in the office and show the estimates you have gotten—several thousand dollars less than what the client is asking. After negotiating a fair deal, you finish up with a flurry of phone calls to the investigator, police, and hospital emergency room personnel. It looks like your hunch about the teenage driver was right, and you make notes that you will use in a follow-up visit to the car owner tomorrow.

Two-Year Training

Some colleges offer an associate's degree or a certificate program in insurance that will help you get licensed in your state. However, many colleges offer only a few courses in insurance, and most do not have a major in the field. Often, insurance companies and insurance associations offer training. The good news is that to prepare yourself for the job of insurance adjuster, it helps to be simply well educated. Business, accounting, communications, negotiation skills, and math are all important areas of study for an adjuster. For example, you might move into an insurance adjuster's position with an associate's degree in business that includes a number of insurance courses.

What to Look For in a School

When you look at colleges, ask yourself these questions:

☞ Does this school offer an insurance major or at least a program of courses that will prepare me for an adjuster's license test in my state?

☞ If this school offers insurance courses but no insurance degree, as is true of many schools, is there someone who can advise me on the best courses to take to become an insurance adjuster?

☞ Does this school offer insurance courses that are in the area I want to pursue?

☞ What kind of job placement record does this school have for insurance adjusters?

☞ How helpful will this school be in helping me obtain an insurance internship?

Did You Know?

The National Insurance Crime Bureau (NICB) estimates that the property-casualty insurance industry pays out about $20 billion a year in fraudulent claims.

In 2003, damage to automobiles from car accidents totaled over $60 billion.

The Future

Insurance is a huge and vital industry. While technology and automation can eliminate some jobs, an adjuster's personal attention can't be replaced. About 263,000 people held jobs as insurance adjusters, appraisers, examiners, or investigators in 2004. Most of these were employed by insurance companies; only a small portion, approximately 2 percent, were self-employed. As our population ages, there will be job growth in the area of medical insurance claims. The other areas of growth probably will be property and casualty insurance. Job opportunities in this field are expected to see healthy growth in the coming years.

Interview with a Professional: Q&A

Jared Stuart

Independent general property adjuster,
Crawford & Company, Los Angeles, California

Q: *How did you get started?*

A: I answered an ad for an assistant for an adjusting company that specializes in property losses. After a couple of months of answering phones, etc., the boss decided to have me apprentice under him because I expressed an interest in getting a state adjuster's license. It was a two-year process, and I eventually passed the state licensing test. Now I am an independent adjuster.

Q: *What is a typical day like?*

A: It's being ready to be called out at a moment's notice and traveling to anywhere in the United States. Once you are there, you download your assignments. Crawford uses a construction software system called Xactware. You make initial contact with the insured, get the facts of the loss, and then schedule an appointment. At the inspection, I take photos and write an estimate of repairs. Back at the office, I write an inspection summary and upload the summary, photos, and estimate to the insurance company that has hired Crawford to adjust the claim.

Q: *What's your advice for those starting a career?*

A: It takes time. There is a lot to learn in terms of estimating the loss and understanding how to read policies. You will either have to go through a training program with a major insurance company or find an individual who owns his own independent adjusting firm. Stay focused on the people—you must have compassion for people going through tremendous upheaval—while at the same time staying focused technically on the job at hand. It is a balancing act.

Q: *What do you like best about being an insurance adjuster?*

A: I like the flexibility of being an independent general adjuster. I work about six months out of the year, and this allows me to spend time with family and friends, and also to travel. I work when there is a catastrophe or natural disaster, and I am paid for each claim that I handle.

Job Seeking Tips

Follow these specific tips for insurance adjusters and turn to Appendix A for help on résumés and interviewing.

✔ Look for jobs posted on insurance companies' Web sites.

✔ Network by joining appropriate business and insurance organizations.

✔ Look for internship opportunities. If you receive an internship, view it as an extended job interview. A successful internship can result in a job offer.

✔ Talk to your career placement counselor.

✔ Emphasize your reasoning skills, trustworthiness, and mathematical abilities in your interviews and cover letters.

"Victor, does our insurance cover sledge-hammer accidents?"
—"Marlene" in the 2002 movie *In-Laws*

Career Connections

For more information, contact the following organizations.

The **National Association of Independent Insurance Adjusters** http://www.naiia.com

The Insurance Guru is a private site about the insurance industry. http://www.the-insurance-guru.com

Adjusters International http://www.adjustersinternational.com

The **American Association of Public Insurance Adjusters** http://www. aapia.org

The **National Association of Public Insurance Adjusters** http://www. napia.com

Information on careers in auto damage appraising can be obtained from:

The **Independent Automotive Damage Appraisers Association** http://www.iada.org

Associate's Degree Programs

Here are a few colleges that offer an associate's degree in business administration with coursework in insurance:

Heartland Community College, Normal, Illinois

Chippewa Valley Technical College, Eau Claire, Wisconsin

Central Georgia Technical College, Macon, Georgia

Daytona Beach Community College, Daytona, Florida

Financial Aid

Inquire about financial aid at the school of your choice. The school itself may offer scholarships or low-interest loans. For more information, turn to Appendix B.

Free online search for scholarships: http://www.fastweb.com/

Related Careers

Some jobs that are similar to the claims adjuster are fire inspector, building inspector, cost estimator, bill and account collector, and medical records claims investigator.

Human Resources Assistant

Vital Statistics

Salary: The median salary is about $31,750. Salaries range from $21,000 to more than $45,780, according to 2006 figures from the U.S. Bureau of Labor Statistics.

Employment: Human resources assistants are as indispensable as ever, and growth in their job numbers is projected to be as fast as the average for all occupations through 2014, according to the Bureau of Labor statistics. Those starting out must grow their computer skills.

Education: An associate's degree in business with a specialty in human resources is best.

Work Environment: Human resources (HR) assistants generally work in a comfortable office environment. Their working hours are the standard 35- to 40-hour week, with few emergencies, if ever. Carpal tunnel syndrome or eyestrain may be a risk if the job requires prolonged computer work.

Are you a person who loves to be around people? Do you handle having a dozen things to do in rapid succession gracefully? If so, you might be ready to become a human resources assistant.

The HR assistant is the person who helps the human resources department run smoothly. If the business is small, the HR assistant will be assigned a wide range of jobs, helping in every aspect of managing employees. This might include job areas such as payroll, health insurance, hiring and firing, working the phones, responding to e-mail, and maintaining records.

In some large companies or organizations, the HR assistant's job may be more specialized. For example, he or she might help only with the recruiting process: placing ads, screening applicants, managing résumés and applications, and writing follow-up letters. In some companies, the HR assistant has a specific title, such as "assignment clerk." The assignment clerk keeps track of new vacancies in the company and informs all company personnel about the job openings; he or she may find qualified candidates and assign them to the new jobs that have become available.

The job outlook for this position is strong. In fact, it is expected that the HR assistant will be given more and more challenging work as businesses move to economize. A candidate who is bilingual in English and Spanish may have an edge in some businesses and geographic areas.

Human resources assistants held about 172,000 jobs in 2004. About 25 percent of HR assistants work for the government, where the pay is generally very good. Many others work for colleges and universities, hospitals, department stores, and banks. You are likely to find an HR job in almost any company that employs more than a few people. The typical salary is around $31,000 to $34,000 but may range as high as $45,000 depending upon the job responsibilities, the geographic location, and the applicant's relevant experience.

No matter what the specifics of the position, this job requires alertness, organization, and discretion. Human resources assistants deal with highly personal employee information, such as salary and health-insurance details, and it is essential that all of this information be kept confidential.

On the Job

Expect a lively atmosphere in an office where you work too hard to get bored; expect to be good and tired at the end of the day. The human resources assistant is a very busy person and may have a wide variety of responsibilities. Depending on the company, the HR assistant may help with employee benefits, maintain health-insurance records, and create and maintain filing systems for personnel. He or she may support recruitment by posting positions, screening applicants, managing the interview schedule, checking references, and writing letters.

The human resources assistant may be responsible for some payroll duties as well. If the company is large enough to provide employee training, the HR assistant may be asked to help with scheduling and oversee materials preparation. When people apply for jobs, often it's the HR assistant who tells them (by phone or by mail) whether or not they got the job, so tact and good communication skills are essential. Sometimes the HR assistant is responsible for details of security. For example, for a defense installation, he or she might be responsible for background checks and verifying information about personnel, vendors, and contractors and be the one to prepare ID cards and badges.

> **"The best HR people are a kind of hybrid: one part pastor, who hears all sins and complaints without recrimination, and one part parent, who loves and nurtures, but gives it to you fast and straight when you're off track."**
> —Jack Welch, former CEO of General Electric

Keys to Success

To be a successful human resources assistant, you should have strong

- people skills
- organizational skills
- communication skills
- computer skills
- discretion

Do You Have What It Takes?

Students who want to go into human resources should enjoy language arts courses as well as talking to people—in person and on the phone. The job requires skilled writing and speaking, clear thinking, and great organization. Most positions also demand computer proficiency in word processing and spreadsheets. The ability to get along with others easily is important, but it is equally important to be firm and to understand employment law. You must be able to keep information confidential. If you are a "people person" and enjoy the challenge of having lots to do every day, this job may be for you.

A Typical Day at Work

It's Monday, and you arrive at the office half an hour early to scroll through e-mails—replies to the job ad you placed for Sunday's classifieds. More e-mail is coming in even as you note possible candidates to interview. Promptly at 9 a.m. two new hires report to the human resources office for their orientation. You explain the health-insurance program, have the new employees fill out a variety of forms, and then take them on a tour of the company's offices, introducing them to people as you go. Throughout the day, you make phone calls, check on job references and backgrounds, take inquiries from employees about vacations and benefits, and answer more e-mails from recruiters. Before lunch, you prepare and format the payroll report and create another report that shows which employees took vacation or sick days. After helping another HR assistant with some filing (paper documentation is important in HR), you meet with a vendor (seller) about the party planned to honor the employees of the month. You've promised yourself you will leave at 5 p.m., but some job interviews run late and you leave the office at 5:30, tired but pleased with everything you accomplished that day.

How to Break In

With the right training and some office experience, it should not be difficult to begin with the job of human resources assistant. Your background should demonstrate that you are good with people and a team player. For example, participating in student government, leading a club, or chairing an event demonstrates organization and people skills. An associate's degree in human resources, skills in computer software such as MS Word and Excel, plus an internship in an HR department will make you a great candidate for the position of human resources assistant.

Two-Year Training

To prepare for the job of HR assistant, an associate's degree in business with a specialty in human resources is best. If that concentration is not available, a degree in business with another concentration, such as management, might also prove useful on the job. Take as many human resources classes as possible. These might include an introductory course on human-resources management. This would cover the principal laws governing hiring, firing, benefits, and work conditions, and other employer responsibilities. Other core courses might focus individually on personnel interviewing, employee relations, staffing a business, compensation, diversity issues, and business writing. It is also important to become proficient in computer software such as word processing and spreadsheet programs. Communications, business writing, psychology, and general office skills are other areas in which to develop skills.

In addition, be sure to get an internship where you will work in a human resources department. A little professional experience in the field goes a long way toward providing you with job-seeking contacts, and the experience you need to open the doors to your career.

What to Look For in a School

When deciding on a two-year school, be sure to ask these questions:

☞ Does this school offer an associate's degree in human resources? Is general human resources taught, or does the program concentrate on one area of human resources, such as recruiting?

☞ Will I learn the necessary computer skills?

☞ Are any of the school's teachers current or former human resources professionals?

☞ How successful has the school been in finding HR internships for the students?

☞ What is the school's job placement rate?

Interview with a Professional:
Q&A
Danielle Little
Human resources assistant, Group Health Inc.,
New York, New York

Q: *How did you get started?*

A: I landed a temporary assignment at a home health care agency in the human resources department. I was given a lot of responsibility. I hired over 80 nurses and 20 administrative assistants for the company's annual immunization program. With that three-month experience, I was able to get my current position.

Q: *What's a typical day like?*

A: Because I support three areas of human resources—benefits, compensation, and recruitment—my responsibilities vary from day to day. I usually arrive between 8:30 and 8:45 to get situated. From 9 to10 a.m., I check my e-mail and respond to questions from employees. I get more e-mails from the recruiters regarding job postings for the day. All jobs have to be posted throughout the building before noon. If the other HR assistant wants to post them, I must sit at the reception desk while he is gone.

No matter what my plan for the day, issues occur and it's imperative that I prioritize. For example, I may have to administer a test for a recruiter, gather data for the director, process departmental transfers immediately, monitor "Accufacts" (background checks), and create various reports—but no matter what, payroll has to be done by 1 p.m. on Mondays.

Q: *What's your advice for those starting a career?*

A: You must have excellent communication skills because you will communicate with people at all levels. You must be enthusiastic and take the initiative. There is an urgency to prove yourself and show that you are capable of performing any and all HR-related tasks. If your manager notices that you have potential, you will be given additional responsibilities, which will help advance your career.

Q: *What's the best part of being a human resources assistant?*

A: You can learn many areas of human resources such as recruitment, benefits, compensation, and employee/labor relations. Every day is different because I am involved in all different areas. This experience is preparing me for the next step in my career, which is to be an HR generalist.

The Future

Even in times of economic downturn, the human resources assistant plays an important and vital function for any business. The demand for this position should remain strong. The HR assistant will continue to handle more complex job functions as automation decreases the need for data entry and increases the need for thoughtful review. For example, the HR assistant of the past might have spent a good deal of time entering data from a paper résumé. Today, that résumé can be submitted online, and the HR assistant may spend more time deciding which candidates to interview than typing in data. As companies grow ever more diverse, human resources assistants also may play a role in coordinating diversity training programs, or helping to handle equal opportunity issues. There are many opportunities for HR assistants in government, health care, finance, insurance, and administrative support services.

Did You Know?

Earnings and benefits have only a 2 percent impact on job satisfaction, while job quality and workplace support have a 70 percent impact, according to a study by the Families and Work Institute.

Job Seeking Tips

See the suggestions below and turn to Appendix A for advice on résumés and interviewing.

✔ Become a model of the person you would like to hire.

✔ Work on interviewing skills, since you will be interviewing others.

✔ Decide on the industry in which you would like to work. You can work for the human resources department in a variety of industries and businesses, or you can work for a recruiting firm.

✔ Ask your internship work supervisor to give you a recommendation.

✔ Join a human resources organization where you will have an opportunity to network as well as expand your job-related knowledge.

✔ Check out *Administratives Assistant* magazine, which is available free through http://www.FreeTradePubs.com.

Career Connections

There are many national and regional human resources professional associations. A few are listed here.

Society for Human Resource Management http://www.shrm.org

World at Work http://www.worldatwork.org

The **International Association for Human Resource Information** http://www.ihrim.org

The **International Public Management Association for Human Resources**. http://www.ipma-hr.org

Associate's Degree Programs

Many colleges offer associate's degrees in business and human resources. Here are a few:

Bryant & Stratton College, Albany, New York

Columbus State Community College, Columbus, Ohio

Manor College, Jenkintown, Pennsylvania

Moraine Valley Community College, Palos Hills, Illinois

Financial Aid

Visit the Web sites of regional human-resources organizations to see if they offer student financial aid. Search on your state or region plus "human resources professional associations." In addition, check out resources in Appendix B of this book.

See "Undergraduate Opportunities" at the **Society for Human Resource Management** Web site for scholarships and financial aid, which include one-time cash scholarships of $1,000. http://www.shrm.org/students/ags_published/

Related Careers

Administrative assistant, receptionist, communications-equipment operators, customer service representative, data processor, and hiring manager.

Loan
Officer

Vital Statistics

Salary: Median annual earnings of loan officers were $48,830, according to 2006 figures from the U.S. Bureau of Labor Statistics. Starting salaries can be less than $27,500, while the top 10 percent earned more than $98,280.

Employment: Though loan officers are in greatest demand when the economy is good, people will always need loans for big-ticket items such as homes, cars, and education. Through 2014 the field is projected to grow more slowly than other occupations, according to the Bureau of Labor Statistics.

Education: A loan officer should have an associate's degree in business with a concentration in finance and credit management. Expect to study business law, economics, and managing credit, as well as how to communicate effectively.

Work Environment: The loan officer often works on the road with a car and laptop. Some loan officers work from an office; others work from home.

A career as a loan officer can be a gamble—a gamble that can pay off well if you are successful. A loan officer is part salesperson, part financial adviser, and part counselor. Usually employed by a commercial bank, savings institution, credit union, or other financial institution, the loan officer finds potential clients who need cash and helps them apply for the right loan. The loan officer also checks into the loan applicant's background, making sure the applicant is financially stable and a good credit risk—someone who is likely to pay back the loan. Some loan officers, usually called "loan consultants," specialize in helping people who have trouble qualifying for a loan.

Most loan officers work in one of three sectors of the economy: real estate (mortgage loans), business (commercial loans), and everything else (consumer loans) including home equity, automobile, and personal loans. The mortgage loan specialist generally gets out of the office a good deal and may even work from a home office. Using a laptop and cell phone, he or she may travel by car to visit the client at a home, office, or building site to complete loan applications. In 2005, mortgage loan officers generally earned between $30,000 and $100,000, according to Robert Half International, a financial services staffing company.

With three years or more of experience, a commercial loan officer (who helps businesses expand or get established) might make up to $100,000. However, depending upon the job and the employer, some of these positions require a four-year bachelor's degree in finance. To work with businesses, the commercial loan officer may travel to other cities and negotiate complex agreements. Of all three types of loan officers, consumer loan officers are most likely to spend most of the workday in the office, usually earning in the range of $30,000 to $50,000 a year.

Compensation for loan officers is usually a combination of a base salary plus commissions (a per-transaction fee). The more loans you make, the more commissions you get.

Two factors give this career its ups and downs: the economy and the number of loans you make each month. When the economy is good and loan rates are low, many people are eager to get loans so the loan officer is very busy, taking on more work in order to make more money. When the economy becomes sluggish and loan rates are high, fewer people want to take loans, and there may be layoffs for loan officers who are not top producers.

When times are good for the economy, to maximize earnings the loan officer may work more than a 40-hour week so he or she can carry as big a "case load" as possible. Some companies expect a minimum number of loans to be made every month. Technology in this area has been developing rapidly, cutting into the job market to some extent by streamlining the application and approval process. However, loan officer positions are still plentiful in all areas of the country, particularly urban and suburban areas where larger financial institutions are often based. Perks may include lower-cost personal loans and free checking. In general, loan officers who work for commission earn more than those who work for salary only, and those who work for larger institutions earn more than those who work for small banks.

On the Job

Depending upon the structure of the finance company, sometimes the loan officer responds to inquiries about loans, and sometimes the loan officer must go out and find business. Finding business may include "cold calling," telephoning individuals or businesses that seem to be likely candidates for a loan and selling the idea over the phone. Sometimes cold calling is not part of the loan officer's job. Instead, the financial institution will have a separate marketing department, and good leads will be passed along to the loan officer to follow up.

When a client is interested in getting a loan, the loan officer guides him or her through the process. The loan officer gets the client's basic information, such as the purpose and amount of the loan required, describes the types of loans for which the client may be eligible, and even helps the client fill out the application. Sometimes this is done over the phone, and sometimes it is done in person.

Once the application is complete, the loan officer needs to analyze and verify the client's information. His or her written notes will be included in the record. Usually, the loan officer will access the client's credit score, which is a computer-generated summary of "credit-worthiness" based on the software's evaluation of a credit history.

Sometimes, if the credit history is unavailable or if there are unusual circumstances in the financial picture, the loan officer will get more financial information from the client and pass the file on to a loan underwriter. The underwriter does a risk assessment, which is included in the client's file. Then the loan officer, probably with his or her manager, decides whether or not to approve the loan.

Networking is usually an important part of the loan officer's job. For example, a mortgage loan officer might create alliances with real-estate brokers in the area. Depending upon the industry in which the loan officer works, he or she will meet and maintain business relations with a variety of agencies and businesses that could supply potential clients.

> **"A bank is a place that will lend you money if you can prove that you don't need it."**
> —Bob Hope, comedian

Keys to Success

To be a successful loan officer, you should have strong
- confidence and persistence
- sales and communication skills
- mathematical and financial sense
- motivation
- integrity

Do You Have What It Takes?

As a loan officer, you are a salesperson as well as a customer-service representative. All day long you will be trying to get people or businesses interested in taking a loan from your institution. The rest of the time you will be investigating their applications. That means a loan officer needs to be a people person. You should enjoy talking on the phone, and you should not be shy about trying to sell a product you believe in. You should be articulate and able to clearly explain information that is difficult for some people to understand.

Because you will be "selling loans," you will encounter rejection. That's where confidence and persistence come in. You cannot be deterred by rejection; it is simply part of a salesperson's job and should be expected. You will also have access to confidential information and must keep it confidential. Because you will be dealing with large sums of money, you may also be subject to a criminal background check. A driver's license is often needed for this job; a sense of humor and good teamwork are important, too.

A Typical Day at Work

First thing in the morning you start making phone calls responding to inquiries that came in via e-mail the night before. You leave a few messages, make notes to call back later, and talk to one person about her desire to refinance her home at a lower interest rate. You haven't gotten out of your pajamas yet, so you shower and dress in conservative business clothes and go on your first appointment of the day. You meet with an elderly couple who want to help finance a condo for their grandson, and you meet with another couple on a possible construction site to advise them about a construction loan.

Your lunch plans include taking a new real estate broker in town out to lunch. You talk to her about your financial institution and how you can work with clients who have "irregular" financial backgrounds to structure mortgages. After lunch, you put in an appearance at the local high school career fair to talk to students about banking-related careers. Later, back at the office, you return telephone calls and follow up on messages you left earlier in the morning. You spend the rest of the day working on your cases, analyzing loan applications and making calls, or using the Internet to verify information.

How to Break in

Two important entrees into this career are the internship and the job placement services at your college. Be sure you are armed with the proper coursework to become a loan officer. Work experience is highly valued; sales jobs and jobs at financial institutions are particularly great experience. Try for an internship as a loan officer or loan officer's assistant. Be sure to highlight on your résumé any sales or customer service experience you have had. If you can not find the ideal job at first, take a customer service job at a financial institution where you would like to be a loan officer and work your way up.

Two-Year Training

An associate's degree in business and finance is available at most two-year colleges. However, some business programs allow students to concentrate in the area of credit management, finance, and banking. For example, Bergen Community College' s two-year degree in business administration with a concentration in banking, credit, and finance is good preparation for the career of loan officer. Typical coursework should include classes in business law, accounting, and credit management as well as communications.

No special credential or certification is required to become a loan officer in a bank or credit union. (Loan officers who work for brokerages or mortgage banks may require a license issued by the state.) However, some professional associations, such as the American Bankers Association and the Mortgage Bankers Association, offer certification for loan officers; some programs require several years of work experience in addition to studying and passing an exam. Becoming certified through one of these professional associations can help a loan officer advance in his or her career. It's also essential to have complete knowledge and an excellent grasp of Microsoft Office (Excel, Word, Access, and PowerPoint).

What to Look For in a School

When looking for a two-year college, ask yourself:

☞ Does this school's associate's degree in business offer a concentration or coursework especially geared toward becoming a loan officer?

☞ Will I learn anything about credit management?

☞ What are the credentials of the teachers? Have they worked in banking, finance, and other business fields?

☞ What kinds of internships will be available to me?

☞ What job placement record does the school have?

The Future

In 2004, there were about 291,000 loan officers working in the United States. Most loan officers worked for financial institutions such as credit unions, savings institutions, or commercial banks.

As with many other careers, technology means change for the loan officer. The increasing use of the Internet for loan applications creates less need for the mortgage broker, and streamlined, automated processes for applications and credit scoring speed the process. The rate of job growth for this career will slow somewhat due to these factors. However, loan officers will still be in greater demand when the economy swings up and interest rates go down. Persons retiring and leaving the industry also will create new job openings. Work experience in sales, banking, and credit management together with pertinent education will give job applicants the edge. It will be important for loan officers to keep current with new types of loans, financial services, and uses of technology.

Interview with a Professional:
Q&A
Brian J. Shropshire
Loan officer, Pine Country Bank, Little Falls, Minnesota

Q: *How did you get started?*

A: My wife knew I wanted to be a banker, so she got me enrolled into the finance and credit management associate' s degree program at Alexandria Technical College. I will just say this: It was tough to make ends meet, but with the drive to succeed, you can do whatever you want to do. After college I networked and was given the opportunity by Pine Country Bank to prove myself as a lender.

Q: *What is a typical day like?*

A: A typical day starts at 8 a.m. Around 9 a.m. we have an interoffice meeting, and then it is off to a real-estate closing, a property inspection, or an appointment with a customer. Otherwise, I'm doing all of the paper work that goes along with lending. Every Wednesday, we loan officers present our loans for the week for approval. I also have responsibilities such as new business development, credit analysis and underwriting, preparing presentations for our loan committee, portfolio management, ongoing customer-relationship management, cross-selling of bank's products and services, and financial analysis. We also have duties outside of the bank, like being involved with Habitat for Humanity and different civic organizations.

Q: *What's your advice for those starting a career?*

A: Make sure you are able to communicate; not just talk, but able to listen and decipher what is said. You need to know math, accounting, and tax preparation. Always be professional no matter where you are, and network as much as possible. The last thing is keep your head up high; you are in charge of your own future. If you keep positive, with the attitude that you can accomplish anything you want to, you will.

Q: *What's the best part of being a loan officer?*

A: I am always up for a challenge, and lending is an absolute challenge. I love my customers, even if some of them from time to time are unhappy with a decision that I have to make. Pine Country Bank is like a big family to me. I honestly have never worked for a place that is this warm, caring, and as family-oriented.

Did You Know?

In 2005, the outstanding mortgages in the United States totaled $10.5 trillion. (Federal Reserve System; Plunkett Research, Ltd.)

Job Seeking Tips

Follow these specific tips for loan officers and turn to Appendix A for help on résumés and interviewing.

✔ Find out if the financial institution provides you with leads. Do they have a telemarketing division, or will you need to do cold calls (calling a stranger)? Will you receive incoming calls?

✔ What will be the minimum number of loans you will need to make each month?

✔ On-the-job training can make your job easier and more profitable. Does the company have a training program?

✔ When starting out, look for a base salary in addition to commissions.

✔ For your first job, look for a well-established financial institution led by experienced managers.

✔ The better the loan terms the company offers, the easier it will be for you to make loans.

Career Connections

For further information, contact the following organizations.

The **National Association of Credit Managers** http://www.nacm.org/

The **Independent Bankers Association** http://www.icba.org/

Associate's Degree Programs

Most colleges offer associate's degrees in business, but not all focus on the career of loan officer. Look for specialties in finance and credit management. Here are a few:

Alexandria Technical College, Alexandria, Minnesota

Bunker Hill Community College, Boston, Massachusetts

Community College of Rhode Island, Warwick, Rhode Island

Ivy Tech Community College: Central Indiana, Indianapolis, Indiana

Financial Aid

Check for scholarships available to business and finance majors with the school of your choice and refer to Appendix B.

Read up on the many sources for business school scholarships at http://www.businessschools.com/articles/scholarships/

Related Careers

Insurance sales agent, real-estate agent, customer service representative, loan counselor, and bank representative.

Court Reporter

Vital Statistics

Salary: Salaries range from $25,000 to more than $80,000 a year; the median yearly salary is $42,920, according to 2006 figures from the U.S. Bureau of Labor Statistics.

Employment: Court reporting in all its forms remains very much in demand and will grow as fast as other occupations through 2014, according to the Bureau of Labor Statistics.

Education: Specialized training in the various forms of court reporting is available at colleges and business schools nationwide.

Work Environment: Court reporters typically work in clean, comfortable settings such as courtrooms, legal offices, convention centers, or television studios.

Well-paid and in demand, court reporters have many different kinds of jobs from which to choose. The most familiar is the reporter using a stenotype machine in a courtroom (think Court TV), making a real-time transcript of the proceedings. But a court reporter may also work in other venues—anyplace where a real-time text record of what is said is needed. That might include business meetings, speeches, lectures, broadcast closed-captioning, Internet text flowing, or real-time translating for the deaf or hard-of-hearing.

Modern technology continues to improve upon the court reporter's job. The basic, familiar method of court reporting employs the stenotype machine. In contrast to someone typing at a regular keyboard, a stenotype machine operator ("stenotypist") presses several keys at once to more quickly create words. However, the words are in a kind of stenographic code, and the stenotypist must learn how to type it and how to decode it to create plain English. Many stenotype machines now use computer-aided transcription, or CAT, to help create the typed transcript.

New technology includes "voice-writing." A hand-held mask containing a microphone shields the court reporter's voice as he or she repeats everything that is said into the voice-writer. Voice-recognition software turns the spoken words into a typescript (which may need to be corrected later on). Another new use of technology, which allows direct recording of different voices as people speak, is called "electronic reporting." The court reporter makes notes while a tape is running to identify who is speaking at which point and to ensure clarity of the transcript. After the proceedings the court reporter transcribes the recording into a text document.

Modern stenotype machines can be hooked up to a computer to produce instantaneous text on a screen, a process called Communication Access Realtime Translation (CART). CART technology is used in television to create instantaneous text (closed-captioning) for the hard-of-hearing. Now that federal mandates require that all new programs from 2006 on be captioned, captioning for television is a growing field. CART can also be used in court, classrooms, and at meetings. In fact, only about a quarter of court reporter jobs actually take place in a courtroom. Many reporters work for the broadcast media, for legal firms, or for the hard-of-hearing.

Learning how to be a court reporter is a challenging task, and setting yourself up in business may require a financial investment for equipment.

On the Job

Court reporting is a highly responsible job. Accuracy is critical. The reporter is the only person present who is trusted to have the complete and actual transcript of what has been said, and important decisions may rest upon what the transcript reports.

While some courts allow electronic recording or voice-recording, the preferred method in court is still stenographic typing. The most difficult of the court reporting skills to learn, stenographic typing, is considered the most accurate and is in highest demand. The reporter in court should expect to work a regular, 40-hour week but must be able to physically and mentally maintain the focus, attention, and stamina to sit and type accurately all day long. Court reporters often help with administrative support to the judge as well, for example by helping to search the record for information. Sometimes the court reporter is paid for the transcription as an additional service, and these transcripts can significantly add to the reporter's income.

Court reporters proficient in CART will qualify for broadcast closed-captioning as well as for other real-time transcription jobs. The reporter who uses the voice-writing method must edit his or her computer-generated translation for correct grammar, accurate identification of proper names and places, and to ensure clarity. The stenotypist must create and maintain a specialized computer dictionary that translates the stenographic strokes into words. Court reporters also must develop a method for filing and storing original notes and files in paper or digital format so they can be easily retrieved if needed.

Court reporters work for government agencies, law offices, broadcast media, and sometimes agencies that supply court reporters as needed. Some reporters work freelance from home offices. Independent contractors and freelancers are more likely to work flexible hours, on-call, part-time, evenings, or weekends. In any case, the reporter is expected to purchase and maintain his or her own equipment, which will usually be customized to the reporter's own methods, quirks, and short cuts. Equipment costs vary widely from $500 to $4,500, depending on whether it's new or used and what the make and model is.

Keys to Success

To be a successful court reporter, you should have

- command of the language
- good hearing
- stenotype or voice writing skills
- good concentration
- ability to meet deadlines
- professional pride in your product

Do You Have What It Takes?

Think about those classes in school where the teacher talked and you had to take notes. Were your notebooks neat and full, the kind other students wanted to borrow when they were absent, or were your pages full of doodles? If you are a good note-taker, if you can listen and write at the same time, courtroom reporting might be a good career for you. Besides being a good listener, you should enjoy working on your own and being self-motivated. You will need good grammar and proofreading skills. You must be able to meet deadlines and you must be accurate. Occasionally, you will need to juggle several different tasks at once, but usually single-minded concentration and accuracy are primary qualifiers for a court reporter.

Familiarity with the jargon of the field (for example, legal terms) and the ability to recognize and spell names or acronyms typically used is also important. Depending upon the job and place of employment, fluency in another language may come in very handy for the court reporter, as well.

> ## "Isn't it funny that anything the Supreme Court says is right?"
> — Robert Frost, poet

How to Break In

If you look for entry-level jobs in the court system, your employer will know that you should start out slow with short assignments. As a freelancer, you might ask local attorneys to use you occasionally for short assignments until they are confident in your abilities. You might also find work at a firm that specializes in placing court reporters. There are a variety of certifications for court reporters, for instance from the National Court Reporters Association, and acquiring certification can take you a long way toward getting a job. Your internship training can also help you gain important experience, and may lead to jobs once your education is complete.

A Typical Day at Work

Your first task of the day will be to check your equipment to make sure everything is working. Also, you must check to see that you have all the supplies and back-up materials you might need. Depending on your place of employment, this may occur at your office or at home before you leave. Once you get to the job site (which could be a courtroom, a newsroom, legal offices, or a lecture hall), you set up your equipment and prepare yourself for action.

As the proceedings unfold, you make an accurate record of everything that is said. That includes comments or emotional responses—sometimes even hand gestures, if required. An attorney may ask for a read back (or a printout if you are doing a real-time transcript), and the proceedings will pause as you comply with the request.

At the end of the day (or whenever your job is finished), you will collect all your gear and head for home—or for the next job if you aren't done for the day. Later, at some point after the job, you may prepare the transcript. Preparing the transcript is less stressful than creating it—you might even prepare it in your pajamas, if you work from home. But wherever you are when you prepare your transcript, you must meet your client's deadline and prepare an accurate transcript.

Two-Year Training

Many private, technical colleges as well as public community colleges offer good programs in court reporting (sometimes called judicial reporting). School curriculums vary, and it will be important to check out the actual courses required for your associate's degree or certificate in court reporting before you decide on a school. Some schools require more general academic classes; others focus more on the technical aspects of court reporting. Some schools focus on the stenotype machine, and others include more training in modern technology.

Basic training includes learning either the stenotype or voice writing machine (or both). Learning how to operate the stenotype machine takes work; once the skills are learned, it takes practice to build up speed and accuracy. Speed and accuracy classes will be part of the required coursework. However, learning stenography should be rewarding when it comes time to look for a job.

In addition to learning the technical skills required, business English and grammar are essential. Other classes may introduce the student to courtroom and legal procedures as well as legal and medical terminology.

Note that most schools will require students to make financial investments in their own equipment. Inquire about the initial cash outlay before you make your commitment. Some places advise buying less expensive machines for school; once on the job, however, you will need to have top quality equipment.

What to Look For in a School

Ask these questions when looking for a two-year school:

☞ Does this school offer training in all of the latest court reporting technologies, or just the stenographic machine?

☞ Does the list of courses seem relevant to your career?

☞ Does the school offer an internship?

☞ Does the school help you find a job?

☞ Is the school accredited by an association recognized by the U.S. Department of Education?

☞ Is the school affiliated with or approved by the National Court Reporters Association? (It does not have to be, but it is a good sign if it is.)

The Future

The future looks great for court reporting. There are more jobs than there are qualified workers. Technology continues to improve, but personal awareness and attention is always needed to operate the machines, polish the transcripts, and ensure accuracy. Furthermore, newer legislation for television and closed-captioning for the hearing-impaired make television transcription more in-demand than ever. Real-time transcription is also needed for deaf and hard-of-hearing students in college and university classes.

In some cases and in some areas of the country, facility with a second language will be especially useful for a court reporter. Don' t be swayed by the lure of easier technology; the stenographic machine will continue to be an important tool, and stenotypists may be in greater demand as fewer people choose to learn the more difficult technology.

Did You Know?

Unlike a regular computer keyboard, a stenotype machine has only 22 keys.

Interview with a Professional:
Q&A

Joanne Mincy

Court reporter, Poughkeepsie, New York

Q: *How did you get started?*

A: I got started in court reporting after I saw how successful my sister was as a court reporter. Since court reporters are in such high demand, I simply went to an agency and told them that I was ready to work. I had already completed an internship, so it was very easy for me to begin working as a freelance reporter. Each day, I call the agency and see where I am assigned for the next day.

Q: *What's a typical day like?*

A: I usually work at lawyers' offices. Once I get to work, which is usually at 10:00 a.m., I set up my equipment (a Stentura 8000LX steno machine) and wait for the deposition to begin. A deposition is oral testimony under oath, and it is conducted in question-and-answer format. Because the testimony is given under oath, I swear the witness in (I'm also a notary public), ask for and record the witness's name and address, and from there the deposition is underway. Usually my day ends in the early to mid afternoon.

Q: *What's your advice for those starting a career?*

A: You need to be a good listener and not easily distracted. In high school and college, you should concentrate on English—court reporters must know grammar and spelling. I'm glad I took a paralegal course in high school, too. Court reporters must have a wealth of knowledge because anything can come up in a deposition so I would recommend legal courses as well as medical courses.

Q: *What's the best part of being a court reporter?*

A: The best part of being a court reporter I would say is the sense of fulfillment, knowing that I have a skill that most people don't have and having the assurance that my job will always be in high demand wherever I go. The hours are good, the freedom is good, and the money is great too.

Job Seeking Tips

Follow these specific tips for court reporters and turn to Appendix A for help on résumés and interviewing.

✔ Use your school internship to get valuable experience and recommendations.

✔ Try getting experience through a court reporter agency.

✔ Become certified by the National Court Reporters Association (guidelines provided at Web site in Career Connections).

✔ The National Court Reporters Association also offers a virtual mentoring program, in which a professional offers advice and encouragement for students in court reporting. Person-to-person mentoring is offered by about 11 state court reporter associations.

✔ To gain experience to put on your résumé, volunteer to provide transcripts of community meetings.

Career Connections

For further information, contact the following organization and check with local job centers of state employment agencies. Also see individual state court reporter associations. And for information on transcription equipment, visit http://www.stenograph.com.

National Court Reporters Association http://www.ncraonline.org

Associate's Degree Programs

Here are some schools offering programs for prospective court reporters:

Clark State Community College, Springfield, Ohio

Community College of Allegheny County, Pittsburgh, Pennsylvania

Lansing Community College, Lansing, Michigan

Financial Aid

Be sure to turn to Appendix B for information on financial aid for two-year students. Here is one source to get you started:

The **National Court Reporters Foundation** http://www.ncraonline .org/foundation

Related Careers

Paralegal, medical transcriptionist, and executive secretary.

Brokerage Assistant

Salary: The median hourly rate is $17 (or about $35,000 a year), according to 2006 figures from the U.S. Bureau of Labor Statistics. The low is around $11 an hour and the high is about $27. Alternatively, some brokerage assistants are paid on a full-time salaried basis and may expect to start at low- to mid-$30,000s with excellent benefits.

Employment: The number of brokerage assistants is projected to grow more slowly than the average for other occupations through 2014, according to the Bureau of Labor Statistics. But this remains a key entry point to the more lucrative and secure financial services positions.

Education: Good preparation for this job is an associate's degree in business and finance, with the option to go on for a bachelor's at a later date.

Work Environment: Brokerage clerks work in a clean, well-lit office environment where the pace is sometimes hectic and stressed.

Sales is an area where success is measured in dollars, and a person's career hinges more on abilities than academic credentials. Nowhere is this more true than in the financial world of securities and commodities trading.

A brokerage clerk is the sales assistant to a stockbroker (also known as a securities and commodities sales agent, a registered representative, an account executive, or a financial consultant). A clerk does not need a broker's license, but it is a real benefit to have one. Because securities brokerage companies often promote from within, becoming a brokerage clerk is a good opportunity to learn the business and move up.

Whatever the title of the job or the specific type of investment sold, the stockbroker is a sales agent, and the brokerage clerk is his or her assistant. The broker, who must develop his or her own list of clients, gives advice to clients about what to buy and sell and how to develop an investment portfolio; the broker also takes buy-and-sell orders from clients and executes the orders through the brokerage firm, usually working on a commission. The brokerage clerk helps with this process.

Brokerage clerks, also known as sales assistants, talk to clients, take orders, and record transactions and other important data. They are involved with much of the daily work that happens in the brokerage firm, and they often have a wide range of responsibilities. Brokerage clerk jobs vary, as do brokers' jobs, and a brokerage clerk may work in operations or even on the trading floor. Most brokers serve individual clients; some serve larger clients such as institutions or pension funds. The size of the firm affects the nature of the job. Some specific positions in larger companies are margin clerk, dividend clerk, and transfer clerk. These brokerage clerks usually don't have client contact; they help to process sales that have been made already.

Newer technology and software programs are making the job of brokerage clerk less paper-oriented and more computer-oriented. Technology and the advent of online trading will make each clerk more productive, so it is expected that this area of employment will not grow rapidly. That means the more prepared you are, the better your chances of employment. Broker jobs, on the other hand, are expected to increase at a healthy pace. An entry-level broker-trainee is often expected to have at least a four-year college degree, but an experienced and successful brokerage clerk with an associate's degree has a good chance of promotion.

Note that insurance agencies and real estate agencies are also called "brokerages." Since the financial services industry has been deregulated, banks, insurance companies, and securities firms compete for business; sales agents' roles and sales products are becoming less distinct. While these other industries offer interesting job opportunities, this chapter concerns the financial services industry, particularly the securities and commodities firms. There are about 5,100 American brokerage firms and 170,000 branch offices, which are regulated by a private company, National Association of Securities Dealers Inc., or NASD, that works closely with and is overseen by the federal Securities and Exchange Commission.

On the Job

Responsibilities vary depending on the job. For example, a *margin clerk* might monitor customer accounts, recording activity and making sure that clients make the appropriate payments and stay within legal boundaries when they purchase stock. A *dividend clerk* will make sure that dividends (interest or pay-outs earned) get paid to clients promptly. A *transfer clerk* makes sure that stock certificates are aligned with banking regulations and may change the security registration upon request from a customer. Someone who makes sure firms and institutions receive and deliver securities quickly and safely is a *receive-and-deliver clerk*; a *purchase-and-sale clerk* will verify stock trades by comparing company records of the selling and buying firms.

Brokerage sales assistants may do some of these job functions as well as a variety of administrative, sales, and clerical duties, usually for two or more brokers. These duties may include helping to arrange scheduling and client meetings, managing the calendar, making travel arrangements, recording important data such as client purchases and sales, maintaining files, creating and updating spreadsheets, and preparing correspondence. The sales assistant often has a good deal of client contact including taking calls, responding to inquiries, explaining the firm's investment products, providing market information, and writing up orders. If a firm sponsors an assistant to study for and take a licensing exam (highly recommended!) such as the Series 7 (see http://www.nasd.com for more information), he or she can also recommend purchases that have been authorized by the broker.

Brokerage clerks generally work a regular 40-hour workweek.

> ## "Don't gamble; take all your savings and buy some good stock and hold it till it goes up, then sell it. If it don't go up, don't buy it."
> —Will Rogers, U.S. humorist & showman (1879–1935)

 ## Keys to Success

To be a successful brokerage assistant you should have

- communication and people skills
- a grasp of financial concepts
- computer skills
- the ability to multitask and follow through on assignments
- self-confidence
- a can-do, cheerful, energetic attitude

Do You Have What It Takes?

To develop a career in the securities industry, you should enjoy a fast-paced environment and do some of your best work when the pressure is on. Teamwork is highly prized, and often co-workers socialize together as well as work together. In fact, socializing is a major part of a broker's ability to develop a client list, so if you hope to advance in this career, you should enjoy getting to know new people in a variety of environments.

You must be organized and attentive to detail because you will have to keep track of a lot of important information. Computer skills are needed (for example, Microsoft Office Suite) but often companies expect to teach new hires their own software programs. Helping the broker with clients is essential, so you must be articulate, friendly, poised, and informed with a good telephone manner. Expect to work independently and take responsibility.

How to Break In

Sales experience is helpful when breaking into this career field, especially jobs in which you have had to go out and sell to strangers. An internship in financial services can be a valuable step toward getting a job as a brokerage clerk. It is helpful to network with everyone you, your family, and friends know to find a first job. After getting your associate's degree, your college placement office should be able to help you find a job.

Since many of the large brokerage firms are based in just a few large cities such as New York, it might be wise to be willing to relocate if a good opportunity comes along. In addition, look for the regional offices of large brokerages, such as Fidelity. There are also jobs available on online brokerage firms such as E*Trade. (However, beware of disreputable online brokerages. Check out any you're interested in online first with your state consumer affairs bureau.) After getting some experience under your belt, don't be afraid to leave a job for a better one if the duties and opportunity don't turn out to be what you expected or what was advertised.

A Typical Day at Work

Your day might begin with telephone work: returning calls from clients, taking orders, resolving problems, answering inquiries from potential clients, and explaining the firms investment opportunities. Next you set up a broker for a meeting with an important client in the conference room, printing out all the relevant information that the broker needs to review before the meeting and reminding her that she has another meeting in the afternoon. You type up correspondence from another broker you support, correcting the grammar and spelling as you go, while continuing to answer the telephones, refer callers to brokers, and help with some questions yourself.

Lunch is a long but interesting event at an upscale restaurant where you have been asked to take notes; your firm's brokerage team is meeting with a corporate client to talk about pension-plan investing. When you return to the office, you spend some time writing a memo to upper management about the meeting, which your immediate boss will review and sign. Several client spreadsheets need to be updated and other papers need to be filed. By the end of the day, you are ready to go out with some fellow sales assistants and brokers to discuss the market and unwind.

Two-Year Training

Most securities and commodities brokerage firms expect to train a new hire on the job, under supervision. Some larger firms have formal training programs, especially for brokers.

There is no specific degree to prepare a brokerage clerk. Some firms require only a high school diploma for the job. However, because the field is becoming increasingly competitive, some college is advisable. Furthermore, the position of sales assistant requires a higher level of education than some of the other purely clerical jobs at the brokerage firm.

An associate's degree in business with a specialty in marketing is useful preparation for the position of brokerage clerk. Be sure to take any available courses on investment securities, and consult with your academic advisor about which courses would help to prepare you for work at a securities firm. If your college does not offer courses on securities and investment, you might try to search for an online class. Choose a college program that can transfer your credits to a four-year school; after you work in the securities field for a time, you then will have the option of getting a B.A. (bachelor of arts) degree if it seems like a good idea.

Useful high school classes include math, public speaking, keyboarding, English, and economics.

What to Look For in a School

Here are some important questions to ask when considering a two-year school:

☞ Does the business program offer training in sales?

☞ Are there any courses in investing and finances?

☞ Will you be able to get an internship with a securities brokerage firm?

☞ Do any teachers have experience in the securities trading field?

☞ If you want to, will you be able to use your associate's degree to go on to a bachelor's degree later on?

The Future

About 75,000 people worked as brokerage clerks in 2004. Almost all of them worked in financial industries such as banks or securities and commodities.

Automation and new technology will increase the amount of work each brokerage clerk can do in a day, thus slowing the growth of the job market. However, positions as securities, commodities, and financial services sales agents are expected to increase at a good pace, and many of these workers will need sales assistants. With a two-year degree, the best career path to take is to become a broker's sales assistant; if desired, you can work toward promotion to the position of broker. Returning to college for a B.A. may help move your career to the higher levels of management.

Did You Know?

In Wall Street slang, a "bucket shop" is any type of brokerage business that is involved in a scam or fraudulent practices.

Interview with a Professional:
Q&A

Caleb Walker

Senior client associate, Merrill Lynch,
Huntsville, Alabama

Q: *How did you get started?*

A: I came from a blue-collar background so my familiarity with the investment world was very limited, but I was always fascinated by how the financial markets worked. I read everything I could about investment and finance. I began to start investing on my own and I wanted to open an IRA account. I called Merrill Lynch, and met with a financial advisor. Noting my interest in financial services, he asked if I would be willing to work one day a week stuffing envelopes. My duties kept increasing until I was hired full time a few months later.

Q: *What's a typical day like?*

A: I come to work before the markets open and check e-mails, voicemail, and review the financial adviser's production from the day before. I will review my notes from the previous day and compose a list of things that need be completed. Once the markets open I spend the majority of my day interacting with clients and addressing their needs.

Q: *What is your advice for those starting a career?*

A: After you have the job, work harder than everyone else. When you are the only assistant early every morning and working late every night, people notice. Then learn everything you can and take any courses you can. As soon as you get hired, try to take the Series 7 and 66 (the entry-level licensing tests for stockbrokers) exams and volunteer for any learning programs that are being offered.

Q: *What do you like best about being a brokerage assistant?*

A: I love the interaction with our clients! When you are dealing with a family's entire life savings you earn a level of trust that makes the clients like your own family. You can really get to know people on a very personal level.

Job Seeking Tips

Follow these specific tips for brokerage clerk and turn to Appendix A for help on résumés and interviewing.

✔ If you aspire to eventually become a broker, look for positions that offer the most client contact and sales support work.

✔ Find out if the firm will sponsor you for a Series 7 license. You will be eligible once you have worked there for four months. The Series 7 license will enable you to assist the broker in making recommendations to clients, and it will make you more marketable.

✔ During your job search, be aware that not all "brokerages" are securities and commodities firms. Some may be insurance or real estate brokerages.

✔ Keep up with financial trends and check a newspaper such as the *Wall Street Journal* regularly.

✔ You may want to check out a broker or a brokerage firm before deciding to work with them. You can do so at http://www.nasd brokercheck.com.

Career Connections

For further information, contact the following professional associations.

National Association of Securities Dealers http://www.nasd.com

North American Securities Administrators Association http://www.NASAA.org

Securities Industry Association http://www.sia.com

Associate's Degree Programs

Many colleges offer associate's degrees in business. Here are a few:

Fox Valley Technical College, Appleton, Wisconsin

Hutchinson Community College, Hutchinson, Kansas

Hudson Valley Community College, Troy, New York

Kent State University, Trumbull Campus, Warren, Ohio

Financial Aid

Check with the college of your choice to see if any scholarships for business students are available, and turn to Appendix B for more information.

Related Careers

Bill and account collectors, bookkeeper, accounting and auditing clerks, order clerk, and bank teller.

Social Services Assistant

Vital Statistics

Salary: Salaries range from $15,480 to $55,000 a year; the median yearly salary is $24,270, according to 2006 figures from the U.S. Bureau of Labor Statistics

Employment: Human services are among the fastest growing fields of employment. Social and human services assistants can choose from an extremely varied assortment of opportunities.

Education: A two-year applied science degree will provide helpful internships and give access to a selection of jobs with better pay.

Work Environment: Employment can be found in clinics, shelters, residential facilities, social services agencies, and hospitals. Some jobs will require at-home visits. A 40-hour work week is typical, and may include some evening and weekend hours.

Helping other people is the common denominator among all jobs in this diverse field. A career in social services can mean many different kinds of work with widely ranging opportunities. A social services assistant may do intake interviews at a rehabilitation hospital, lead a group at a nursing home, perform administrative work at a social service agency, deliver food to the elderly, or assist at a nursery school or day-care facility. Human service workers are trained to be generalists, people helpers in a people-helping field. Having so many different choices means that you can choose the job that most suits your goals and temperament.

Social services assistants often work closely with a supervising social worker to provide support and help with screening, intervention, and documentation of people who come to a social services agency looking for help.

Most jobs revolve around patient care and advocacy. As a social services assistant, you might monitor and supervise people in need, or help them get the services that will allow them to live the best lives they can achieve. You may help clients enhance the quality of life by offering them more independence and a higher level of functioning.

Depending upon the environment, social and human services assistants work under different degrees of supervision; frequently they are part of a care-giving team. The assistant may work in settings ranging from clinics and hospitals to social services agencies and residential facilities. Some of the work, such as visiting clients at home, may be dangerous. Many of the jobs in this field can be emotionally demanding, but the potential for satisfaction in this career is substantial.

Many jobs in this field involve working with people who are vulnerable in various ways. Group home workers may be required to hold a valid driver's license and undergo a criminal background check.

Internships are a standard part of the educational process and are an excellent way to explore the many diverse opportunities this field offers. They are also pathways to employment, as interns are frequently offered jobs by the agency they've interned with. Promotion potential from within an agency is high, and entry-level workers in this field often continue their education in order to get higher-level jobs. Going on for a bachelor's or master's degree will qualify a social services assistant for supervisory and administrative positions in fields like mental health, social work, counseling, and education.

The demand for social services assistants is currently high and climbing higher, especially for those with appropriate education and training. Long-term worker turnover, a growing elderly population, and a never-ending stream of people in need all contribute to a continuously expanding field. As long as there are people, there will be a need for people helpers.

A person's degree of education strongly influences the work assignments in this field; those with only a high school degree are often assigned to direct-care jobs, while those with college degrees work more in supportive and management positions.

Though entry-level pay is low, people in this field usually have a passion for their career; rarely is it "just a job." If working in a helping field interests you, working as a human services assistant is an excellent way to get a start in this emotionally demanding yet rewarding profession.

On the Job

Though a job as a social services assistant is not usually very physically demanding, it frequently is emotionally demanding. Your clients may be people with developmental or emotional disabilities who at times require patience and skill. For instance, you may work with abused children in a residence or former drug-users in a treatment facility. Workers at group homes may be required to undergo a criminal background check and fingerprinting. Work at residential facilities often necessitates overnight and weekend hours, which can be schedule-disrupting and fatiguing. What's more, at-home visits can be unpredictable and even dangerous though most agencies go to great lengths to ensure safety. You will be called on at times to be the ultimate multitasker as you juggle your client's needs, work with a supervisory team, and handle required paperwork.

Working conditions vary; you may be employed in an office, a group home, a day-care facility or a clinic. Many social services assistants are closely supervised and work as part of team. You will often be expected to keep excellent records of client care and interaction and attend frequent meetings to plan and assess client progress.

Sometimes social service agencies are short-staffed, and you will be asked to handle many tasks at once. A well-developed sense of responsibility, patience, and compassion are important personal assets. Expect to get on-the-job and in-service training, such as attending seminars and workshops.

> **"To give real service you must add something that cannot be bought or measured with money, and that is sincerity and integrity."**
> —Douglas Adams, author

Keys to Success

To be a successful social services assistant, you should have

- a genuine concern for the well-being of others
- an excellent ability to communicate
- patience
- a strong sense of responsibility
- the ability to manage time effectively
- the ability to work as part of a team
- good organizational skills

Do You Have What It Takes?

Do friends often turn to you for advice? Do you genuinely like people? When you know that someone is in trouble, do you feel a strong desire to help him or her? Personal qualities such as compassion and patience as well as good communication skills and the ability to work well with others are important for those who work in this field. High school classes in psychology, social studies, biology, and chemistry will be useful. Because filling out paperwork will be a part of most jobs, good writing skills are helpful as well.

How to Break In

Due to the continuing high demand for workers in this field, it's not difficult for even minimally educated workers to find employment in places like residential facilities, a typical source of entry-level jobs. For the less stressful and better paying jobs, however, post-high school education is a must.

Spending volunteer hours at a social-services institution before looking for a job will provide important hands-on experience and will be attractive to future employers. College internships are enormously instructive and will frequently lead to employment as well. Advancement often happens from within an organization, and furthering your education helps enhance the prospects of promotion.

A Typical Day at Work

A typical day in the social services field revolves around helping clients get their needs met, whether the needs are emotional or physical. As a social services assistant who works at a human services agency, you may start your day by meeting with the rest of your client support team, which may include a supervising social worker, a psychologist, and a physical or occupational therapist. Your roster of clients will be discussed and their treatment plans fine-tuned. Next on your schedule is an intake interview with a new client, which will include assessing her eligibility for food stamps and Medicaid and temporary welfare assistance. Following that, you might facilitate a group focused on teaching job-finding skills to welfare recipients. You'll spend some time filling out and filing paperwork, and then call several clients to make sure they're taking prescribed medication or to ask if they need transportation to a scheduled appointment or treatment program. You might then drive to another client's residence to assess his living situation and talk with him about treatment goals, and end the day by returning to the office to finish filing papers.

Two-Year Training

An associate's degree in applied science will qualify you for many entry-level positions in public and private sector human services agencies. A degree program in human services will provide essential education and hands-on training for employment in this field.

You will receive training in skills such as patient observation and methods for conducting interviews, record keeping, administrative training, implementing plans of treatment, handling crises, problem solving, and appropriate management procedures. The curriculum will include courses in the humanities, science, and liberal arts. Psychology classes will be helpful, and in most schools you'll have the opportunity to focus your course of study on one particular aspect of the field, such as child protection, gerontology (a specialty in aging), or addiction. Most programs require an internship for graduation; some require the completion of several. Many educational institutions will require potential students to undergo a criminal background check.

What to Look For in a School

Ask these important questions when choosing a school:

☞ Do instructors have plenty of experience in the field?

☞ Does the program offer good internship opportunities? (More than one is optimal.)

☞ Does the program offer a strong core curriculum?

☞ Does the training include a wide range of applicable skills?

☞ Is the program accredited by the CSHSE (Council for Standards for Human Services Education)?

☞ Does the program enable you to specialize in an area of interest, such as gerontology?

☞ Does the program have partnerships with local human service organizations?

☞ Is the program's focus more on client-handling skills, supervisory ones, or a balance of both?

The Future

The outlook for employment in social services is outstanding. Social services is one of the fastest growing occupational fields and is predicted to increase more rapidly than any others in the early decades of the 21st century. This will partly be due to retiring, advancing, and departing workers but will also be caused by an ever-increasing demand for social and human services.

Downsizing and cost-controls have created a trend toward hiring human and social services assistants for jobs formerly filled by social workers. Competition will be keenest in urban areas, but job opportunities will abound in rural regions as well as cities. Work also will be abundant in private sector jobs as state and local government agencies increasingly outsource services to trim costs. Growing need will be seen for help with populations such as the elderly, people in residential facilities, pregnant teenagers, substance abusers, and the developmentally challenged and mentally ill.

Did You Know?

The human services career field had its start in a 1950s trend to take the mentally ill out of large impersonal institutions and help them live in society.

Interview with a Professional:
Q&A
Deb Weir

Social services assistant, Lexington Center
for Recovery, Poughkeepsie, New York

Q: *How did you get started?*

A: I was lecturing on domestic violence but I did not have academic credentials. I asked at the local community college about a degree I could get that would provide me with these credentials, and they signed me up for an associate's degree in social services with the CASAC (certificate in alcoholism and substance abuse counseling) program. Though I didn't finish the associate's degree, I did get the CASAC. Once in the field, I found I loved working with people with addictions.

Q: *What's a typical day like?*

A: One of the reasons I love this field is because no two days are exactly alike. Most days involve running a group therapy session, one or two individual therapy sessions, doing drug testing, and handling paperwork, but there are some very intense variables. Our clients can become unstable, and it's not uncommon for people to arrive for treatment intoxicated or high, which radically changes how the individual is handled.

Q: *What is your advice for those starting a career?*

A: If you are considering a career in this field, my advice would be to first carefully examine your motives. Many people get into this field because they are themselves in recovery, or a family member was an addict. And while that may give you added knowledge or an insider's perspective, working with alcoholics and addicts is *not* a substitute for taking care of your own self-help or support. This job is emotionally draining and there's a low success rate for the clients and a high burnout rate for counselors. The best counselors are those who do not personalize their client's problems or behaviors.

Q: *What is the best part of being a social services assistant?*

A: The best part is also the part that is rarest; watching a client "get it." It's magical to be a part of their lives when they start wanting to change so much that they are willing to go through the pain of recovery.

Job Seeking Tips

Follow these specific tips for social services assistants and turn to Appendix A for help on résumés and interviewing.

✔ Invest time in volunteering or serving an internship.

✔ Working at a residential facility will provide a good introduction to the field.

✔ Demonstrate a high degree of patience, compassion, and desire to help others in your job interviews. Employers value this.

✔ Good record-keeping skills can be as important as strong people skills.

✔ If you're unsure of your main area of interest, emphasize a variety of experiences and versatility in your résumés.

Career Connections

For further information, contact the following organizations.

The **National Organization for Human Services** offers a Web site with a job board, educational information, regional links, and much more. http://www.nohse.org

The **National Human Services Assembly** is an organization of leading social services agencies around the United States. The site includes information about jobs, awards, conferences, and more.   http://www.nassembly.org

The **Alliance for Children and Families** is an organization for professionals and other groups focused on advocacy for children and families.   http://www.alliance1.org

For more information, search online for regional organizations in your area of interest, whether it's corrections, the elderly, drug rehabilitation, or foster care. Many associations exist in specialized social service interest areas.

Associate's Degree Programs

Each of America's fifty states as well as Canada and Australia offer college programs in human services—New York State, in fact, offers more than 20.

Here's a selection of programs around the United States:

Hillsborough Community College, Tampa, Florida

Hudson Valley Community College, Troy, New York

Terra Community College, Fremont, Ohio

Community College of Denver, Denver, Colorado

Financial Aid

Many colleges offer scholarships to students in the human services field, such as the one offered by Arizona State University (Tempe, Arizona) for human services majors enrolled full or part time with a minimum 3.5 grade point average (GPA). See Appendix B for financial aid information.

The NOHS offers the David Maloney scholarship nationally to student members of their organization with a 3.0 or better GPA. http://www.nationalhumanservices.org/scholarship.html

Related Careers

Social worker, therapist, childcare worker, home health aide, nursing and psychiatric aide, counselor, occupational therapy assistant, and physical therapist aide.

Executive Assistant or Executive Secretary

Vital Statistics

Salary: Depending on the company, salaries can range from $30,000 to about $65,000. Median annual earnings for executive secretaries and administrative assistants are about $35,000, according to 2006 figures from the U.S. Bureau of Labor Statistics.

Employment: This is a vast job market, likely to remain stable while growing more slowly than other occupations through 2014, according to the Bureau of Labor Statistics.

Education: A valuable two-year degree to get is an associate's in business with a concentration in executive assistant or executive secretary technology.

Work Environment: Executive assistants work in an office in support of top company executives, so their working environment is usually top level.

"Secretary?" It may be an old-fashioned word, but it is a thoroughly contemporary job for the man or woman in business. Also known as executive assistant, the executive secretary is often the boss of other support staff and usually the right hand of the company's top executives. Spell executive assistant/secretary: *i-n-d-i-s-p-e-n-s-a-b-l-e*. This is a highly responsible and stable position, usually commanding a good salary and benefits.

In the days of computer technology, executives do much of the work that secretaries used to do—such as keyboarding—and executive secretaries do more in the area of management. An executive assistant may pinch-hit for the boss when he or she is away: knowing how to answer questions, deal with small emergencies, and when the situation is critical enough, phone the head honcho. The executive secretary is likely to spend less time on clerical tasks such as typing and filing and more on organizational and management tasks, such as planning meetings, hiring staff, and creating reports. On the other hand, the executive assistant might also proofread and retype a speech or reorganize a client's files. The key is flexibility: doing whatever is needed to assist the executive to whom you are assigned.

Many jobs carry the title of "administrative assistant." While this job may be a stepping-stone to becoming an executive assistant, it is not the same job. The administrative assistant is usually hired to perform the less-skilled clerical tasks, such as filing, keyboarding, data entry, photocopying, and answering phones. While the executive assistant may perform some of these tasks, he or she will do them within the context of a much larger overall responsibility.

The executive assistant is usually hired by the company and assigned to an executive. Therefore he or she remains with the company and with the position even when the boss leaves or changes jobs. In fact, the executive assistant may be the person who holds it all together for others in the company in times of change and transition. When the new boss needs to get acclimated to the job, it's the executive assistant who shows him or her how things work in the company. The executive assistant is the one who knows where everything is and how everything works. While he or she may not make the executive decisions, the assistant often helps the boss make the right decisions. It's been said that the executive assistant is office manager, accountant, and secretarial clerk all rolled up into one. To be the right-hand person to the vice-president or CEO (chief executive officer) of a company, the executive assistant must be flexible, savvy, and committed. Often assigned to support more than one position, the executive assistant must also be an able multitasker.

> **"Accomplishing the impossible means only that the boss will add it to your regular duties."**
> —Doug Larson, cartoonist

On the Job

The executive assistant must be able to communicate effectively and tactfully when called upon to interact with clients, staff, and top executives. Responsibilities usually will include scheduling meetings and appointments, making travel arrangements, maintaining the executive's calendar, preparing correspondence and reports, monitoring budgets, and working on special projects.

The job may also require answering telephones and helping with correspondence, especially e-mail. The executive assistant must be able to use good grammar and spelling. These skills may be used to prepare a Microsoft Office Suite PowerPoint presentation for the boss, write a letter to a client, or review and proofread an internal newsletter. Fluency in a second language can be useful for multinational corporations or for companies that employ a diverse workforce.

Depending on the company, the executive assistant may have a variety of other responsibilities. For example, he or she might have broad fiscal duties such as billing, bookkeeping, or overseeing these jobs. Other jobs may include screening mail and telephone calls and creating priorities for the boss's attention; preparing and tracking expense reports; following up on inquiries or assignments, delegating work, and making sure everything gets done; hiring and managing temporary or contract staff; and training staff where needed.

Keys to Success

To be a successful executive secretary, you should have

- poise and self-confidence
- the ability to anticipate your boss's needs
- leadership skills
- time-management skills
- oral and written communication skills
- flexibility and patience
- computer skills

Do You Have What It Takes?

Executive secretary is the kind of job where you take the assignment given to you and run with it. You will not be the type who does the minimum. If you do a job, you make sure it is done right. If you see that something is needed, you like to take care of it yourself.

Working well with others is essential, and that means having great communication, empathy, tact, and firmness. Much of the job is helping someone else manage a complex and demanding business; you must be able to anticipate what the boss needs as well as maintain such good organization that everything is at your fingertips with a moment's notice.

Independence and taking responsibility are good qualities for the executive assistant to have. Often you may be called upon to be a leader in the absence of your boss, and you may need to pinch-hit when the boss is working on another project. At the same time certain concrete and specific skills are needed, in particular, the use of the Microsoft Office Suite or a similar set of skills: fast, accurate typing (45-60 words a minute), and experience with spreadsheets, databases, Internet skills, and computer presentations such as PowerPoint. Understanding how to organize and file both online and paper documents—the crucial job of information management—is also essential. The executive assistant, after all, will be the ultimate resource when questions arise. Finally, as a higher-up in your company or organization, you must have discretion. You will be likely to handle information that must be kept confidential.

A Typical Day at Work

When you arrive for the day, the boss is in a meeting uptown and an unscheduled client is waiting. You cover for your boss, reassure the client, and schedule a meeting with your boss for later in the week. Next you respond to the boss's e-mails, pass along the important ones, and sort through the mail.

Before your boss returns you go into the conference room and put the finishing touches on her presentation, running through all of the slides to make sure they are effective and make the important points. When your boss gets back you take her through the presentation, and you make the changes she asks for. Later you and your boss meet with two department vice-presidents to discuss the launch of a new product line. You take notes and type these up and send around the conference report in an e-mail.

Before the day ends you need to review the books and make sure the accounts payable report will be finished on time. You compose and type up a letter to a client about a problem that has been solved, and sign for your boss (using your own name and title). Before leaving you check the appointments for tomorrow and make sure everyone knows where they are supposed to be.

How to Break In

Most senior executive assistants have experience on the job. Expect to break in at a lower level and work your way up. It will be critical to get a good internship; the more highly the person you assist is placed in the corporate structure, the better. Straight secretarial experience translates well to the executive assistant position, especially with the right skills in place. Be sure to find a job where there is opportunity for added responsibility and advancement. Once on the job, take the initiative and show you are capable of thinking for yourself . . . and for your boss.

Did You Know?

An executive secretary in the 1950s, Bette Nesmith Graham, invented Liquid Paper, the original "White Out."

Two-Year Training

Although a short-term secretarial course or skills learned in high school used to qualify workers for this position, now employers expect to see an associate's degree in business or even a bachelor's. A good two-year program with a specialty in executive assistant technology is good preparation for this career. Expect to study business math, business law, English, accounting, and management. Good writing, spelling, grammar, and proofreading skills are essential. Equally important are financial and computer skills. Become expert with word-processing, presentation, and spreadsheet software programs. Practice keyboarding up to 60 words per minute or better.

What to Look For in a School

When considering a two-year school, be sure to ask these questions:

☞ Does the school distinguish between an administrative assistant and an executive assistant?

☞ Does the school have a business concentration in executive assistant technology?

☞ What is the school's internship and job-placement record? How well are graduates placed, and how quickly do they advance? Do interns get any contact with corporate executives?

☞ Will the business program train you in the important computer software applications, business English, business math, and management skills?

The Future

Over 1.5 million people in the United States work as executive assistants, and almost 2 million more work as secretaries. While the number of secretarial positions available may increase slowly, job growth in the area of the executive assistant is expected to remain healthy. High growth industries such as health care, social services, and legal services mean more executive assistant openings in the specialized areas of medicine and law. Other industries where growth is anticipated are the sciences and professional and technical services, along with private educational institutions.

Undoubtedly, emerging technology will continue to influence the shape and size of the executive assistant's job. However, the tact, consideration, forethought, and leadership that characterize the executive assistant cannot be automated. This position will continue to be essential.

Job Seeking Tips

Follow these specific tips for executive assistants and turn to Appendix A for help on résumés and interviewing.

✔ Be sure your keyboarding rate is 45 words per minute at a minimum.

✔ Be sure you can list relevant software applications that you know.

✔ On your résumé or cover letter, emphasize any executives you have helped and any management responsibilities you have had.

✔ In school look for internships or volunteer opportunities assisting an executive secretary.

✔ Describe something you did that exhibits superior time management or organization.

✔ Fluency in a foreign language, especially writing abilities, can be a real asset. Look for a firm that can use your skills.

✔ Check out magazines such as *Executive Secretary* and *Administrative Assistant Magazine,* which are available free through FreeTradePubs.com

Interview with a Professional:
Q&A
Zenaida Martinez
Executive secretary, New York, New York

Q: *How did you get started?*

A. I got my first job as a receptionist/secretary through an agency. I used the job to build my work experience and my skills. My past managers often let me run their offices; they trusted my knowledge and professionalism.

Q: *What's a typical day like?*

A: A typical day for me consists of answering phones and giving administrative support to my supervisor, the people reporting directly to him, and their staffs. I have daily, weekly, and monthly reports that I create for management.

Through my reports management can see how the department is doing and what may need to be corrected. I also make sure that the office is running smoothly. Be aware: You can have your whole day planned, and you may have to just drop whatever you are doing because something urgent comes up.

Q: *What's your advice for those starting a career?*

A: College internships help very much when you are looking for work. Make sure that the career path you choose is one that you will enjoy and feel proud of. Take pride in everything you do, and at the end of the day you will feel a sense of accomplishment. To advance quickly in this field, keep a professional attitude at all times and always try to keep your skills sharp and up-to-date. For example, if there is a new software program on the market, take a course on it. Learn as much as you can about the company you work for, too.

Q: *What's the best part of being an executive assistant/executive secretary?*

A: I really enjoy when I'm asked to create a report or even a presentation. I get to put my knowledge to work. But the best part of my job is the group of people I work with. They are very professional, knowledgeable, and I learn something new from them every day.

Career Connections

For further information, contact the following organizations.

The **National Association for Female Executives**
http://www.nafe.com

The **National Association of Executive Secretaries**
http://www.naesaa.com/

The **International Association of Administrative Professionals**
http://www.iaap-hq.org/

Associate's Degree Programs

Many colleges offer associate's degrees in business, but not all offer a concentration in becoming an executive assistant. Here are a few that do:

Daymar College, Louisville, Newport, and Owensboro, Kentucky

Cincinati State Technical & Community College, Cincinnati, Ohio

Dakota County Technical College, Rosemount, Minnesota

Grossmont Community College, El Cajon, California

Financial Aid

Look for scholarships at the school of your choice. Also check the local chapters of the National Association of Executive Secretaries. For more on financial aid for two-year students, turn to Appendix B.

Related Careers

Office manager, administrative assistant, accounts payable/receivable manager, bookkeeper, paralegal, and medical assistant.

Sports and Fitness Manager

Vital Statistics

Salary: Salaries range from $14,530 to around $55,560. The median salary is $25,470, according to 2006 figures from the U.S. Bureau of Labor Statistics.

Employment: The business of fitness and health has grown substantially over the past two decades and is projected to continue growing at a much-faster-than-average rate.

Education: A degree or certificate in sport and fitness management is good preparation for work in recreation, health, and fitness centers. A certificate can be completed within a year, but employers are increasingly favoring candidates with an associate's degree. Additional training, such as personal trainer certification, is also helpful.

Work Environment: Your work environment will be an indoor recreational facility that may be public or private. Health and fitness clubs can be all sizes, from small, individually owned establishments to large franchises.

Versatile, upbeat, friendly, and helpful—that's the personality profile of a sports and fitness manager.

If you're passionate about sport and fitness training, this job could be a dream come true. Your workplace will be the place where others come to play; you'll earn your living in a business centered on health and well-being. Many who manage health and fitness clubs have come to this field through a strong personal interest such as team or individual sports; for most of them, fitness plays a featured role in their lives.

Employment possibilities are large and varied and can range from managing a private health club facility to coordinating fitness at a large corporation. A sports and fitness club manager's job includes overseeing many facets of the business's operations as well as ways of meeting the needs of the fitness-seeking public and specific groups within it. Responsibilities may include marketing and sales, as well as creating programs and promotional material such as flyers and newsletters.

You may also be responsible for hiring, firing, training, and overseeing staff; handling payroll; selecting equipment and monitoring its upkeep; and creating, staffing, and overseeing program development. Selecting and overseeing health maintenance facilities such as a weight room and cardiovascular equipment may be your responsibility, as well as managing fitness classes such as aerobics and Pilates.

The ability to work well with people should be high on your skill list; you'll be the main "friendly face" for the business you work for. Excellent communication skills are important. You may be called on to fill in for every duty in the facility, including answering the phone, managing the front desk, greeting clients, selling memberships, giving tours, and orienting new arrivals.

An increasing awareness of the value of physical fitness has led to interest in bringing health and fitness principles to a wider-than-ever segment of the population; clients may include those with special needs, senior citizens, school children, and corporate employees. It's important for a sports and fitness manager to be able to work with every kind of person, without bias or prejudice.

Some fitness center directors may also serve as trainers and group exercise instructors. Knowledge of fitness training is increasingly important for this job; many sports and fitness managers also have personal trainer certification. CPR certification is also essential, as is experience in assessing a client's fitness levels and creating appropriate workout programs.

On the Job

Sports and fitness club managers are called to perform a wide variety of tasks, which can include everything from office skills to equipment maintenance. You are a jack-of-all-trades. You'll be the person who trains new employees, handles customers' comments and complaints, critiques and praises employees, and acts as go-between for staff and owner. In other words, a good sports and fitness manager will be the glue that binds the facility together; the one expected to know everything from where the spare key for the sauna is kept to whom to call when the heat won't go on or a Nautilus machine breaks down. Because you'll be in a place that emphasizes physical well-being, you'll be expected to have excellent knowledge of exercise machines and how to correctly use them. This is not a chair-sitting sort of workplace; an active job calls for an active person. You should be flexible-minded and in reasonably good physical shape. You might be asked to demonstrate machine use, man the desk, handle sales and registrations, register new clients and manage the staff—wherever there's a need is where you'll go.

Though your work environment will generally be a comfortable one— an indoor facility that's climate-controlled for the comfort of customers and workers—there is danger of injury in exercise and the use of exercise machines. You'll need to know the basics of emergency medicine. CPR certification is mandatory in some facilities.

You may be called on to travel between several locations, as well as work some holidays, evenings, and weekends. Work in this field is sometimes part-time, which may affect benefits such as health insurance. Unlimited use of the facilities, however, is usually included with the job.

Keys to Success

To be a successful sport and fitness manager, you should have

- ⚷ interest and knowledge in health and fitness
- ⚷ organizational ability
- ⚷ managerial skills
- ⚷ communication skills
- ⚷ sensitivity to others' needs
- ⚷ ability to motivate

Do You Have What It Takes?

If you have a keen interest in health and excellent organizational and management skills, this could be the right career for you. Fitness club managers should be reasonably athletic and in good health. Leadership skills are important and so is a broad knowledge of the function and physiology of the human body. A genuine liking for people is essential, as is an ability to work with people of different backgrounds, ages, and ability levels. Good fitness club managers are like cheerleaders for the world of health and fitness—people who can motivate and inspire others who work with and for them.

A Typical Day at Work

A sports and fitness club manager is the most responsible person in a facility—you may be the first to arrive and the last one to leave. A typical day may start with business details; you take care of contracts and make sure membership packages are up to date. Next you turn your attention to the employees. You look over the personal training and class schedule and make sure everyone knows what they're supposed to be doing and when. If the front desk associate is out, you'll take over that job and spend time answering the phones and dealing with customers' comments and needs. When someone walks in and asks about the facility, you'll lead them on a tour and give them a brochure and price list.

The facility will need your attention too. If someone misplaces the key to the weight room, you'll locate the extra one. If there's a clog in one of the drains in the shower room, you'll find a plumber who can come out right away.

The day may end with more business details. If it's payroll day, you'll make out employee checks. Before you leave, you run through your own weight-training routine, and then look over the next day's schedule so you can be organized tomorrow.

How To Break In

Many fitness and sport club managers get into the business because of a personal interest in health and fitness. A passion for sports and sports training is a very good beginning to finding a place for yourself in this exciting field.

On-the-job training is important. Part-time jobs at fitness centers are generally plentiful and provide an excellent way to become familiar with this career; many sport and fitness club managers start as assistants and work their way up through an organization as they acquire on-the-job training.

Possessing a personal trainer's certificate is a plus in the eyes of employers; so are good business and accounting skills. Knowledge of the human body and how to train it is extremely important; the best sport and fitness managers have also spent time as trainers or instructors.

> **"You have to stay in shape. My grandmother, she started walking five miles a day when she was 60. She's 97 today, and we don't know where the heck she is."**
> —Ellen Degeneres, comedian

Two-Year Training

It is not essential to have a college degree to become a sports and fitness manager, but it's an asset that's becoming increasingly more important in this field. Different tiers of training are available. Some college programs offer a "certificate of proficiency," which is an option that can get you on your way in less than two years. An associate of science degree with a sport and fitness management concentration is formulated to prepare you directly for this marketplace. Some colleges offer more options than one degree, so choose the one that best suits your needs. An associate's degree or certificate will allow immediate work in a fitness or health center. (For most upper-level management jobs such as sports team manager, a bachelor's degree is required, and to teach sports and fitness curriculum at college level, you'll need a master's or doctorate.)

Many colleges offer associate's degrees or certificates in sport and fitness management. Courses will include an overview of the history of the industry, as well as instruction in marketing, sales, management and business, health and safety standards, and public relations. Some programs require business math courses such as statistics and economics.

Good communication and business skills are essential, so helpful high school preparation for this career will feature courses in English and math. You'll be responsible for managing people and mediating conflict as well as helping people train their bodies, so you'll need to understand what makes them tick both mentally and physically; courses in psychology, social studies, and physics will be useful. Physical education courses are a must, and classes in safety and first aid will be a plus, as will be studying a second language. Courses in business math skills, such as economics and statistics, are required by some colleges.

What to Look For in a School

These are important questions to ask when choosing a school:

☞ Does the school offer internships?

☞ Have the instructors worked as managers in the field of sport and fitness?

☞ Does the school help with job placement?

☞ Is the coursework well-rounded to include classes in finance and business management?

☞ What is the school's job placement history?

The Future

People's awareness of the need to actively work on their health and fitness is steadily increasing; the desire for the health-insurance industry to cut costs by promoting fitness is growing along with the number of people willing to spend more time and money on fitness. What's more, the escalating numbers of adult and childhood obesity in America show a need for health and fitness providers that is still unmet; this industry is rapidly growing and predicted to stay that way.

Part of the reason for projected future growth in this industry is the incredible diversity opening to workers in this field. Sports and fitness workers can be employed in public or private companies, work with populations such as the elderly, school children, or special-needs individuals, and in recreation, health, sports and fitness centers, or spas.

Did You Know?

Exercise can make you smarter: Physically active kids perform better academically, according to the California Department of Education.

Interview with a Professional:
Q&A
Justin Schulman

Owner, My Fitness Trainer, Natick, Massachusetts

Q: *How did you get started?*

A: After I got certified as a personal trainer, I immediately opened the yellow pages and started calling every number listed under health/fitness, inquiring about available positions. I got several part-time training positions, which included some membership duties. After a little while I felt I could put together a better personal training/fitness program. Luckily, I was able to convince one of my gym owners that I was right. I hired a staff and created systems to handle the day-to-day fitness operations of the facility. My ultimate goal was to open my own facility, and I was able to do just that.

Q: *What's a typical day like?*

A: I arrive at work early (think: sun not out yet!) and look at the day's schedule and the tasks that need attention. Then I inspect the facilities for cleanliness. Once the staff arrives, I brief everyone on what needs to be accomplished in addition to training their clients. In between training my own clients, I return calls of new potential members and schedule their first visits. I arrange direct-mail mailings, make sure the staff has business cards and that there are sufficient forms and marketing materials available. I also call the equipment maintenance company for repairs and maintenance.

I often spend time creating and implementing systems. Everything from how the phones are to be answered to how the towels are folded is documented and explained to the staff. Feedback from the staff and members is used to make these systems work better.

Q: *What's your advice for those starting a career?*

A: Get a schedule book and use it. Systemize and document the tasks that you and your staff do regularly to create standards. Once this is done, spend your time making sure the staff understands the standards, or you will spend your time following them around re-doing everything "the right way."

Q: *What's the best part of being a sports and fitness manager?*

A: You get to shape and create a whole culture within a facility. The decisions you make about staffing, marketing, sales approaches, programs, even uniforms define the member experience, and that is the difference between a successful facility and an unsuccessful one.

Job Seeking Tips

Follow these specific tips for sport and fitness managers and refer to Appendix A for help on résumés and interviewing.

✔ Start by working various jobs at a health and fitness facility.

✔ To impress employers, create a versatile resume that demonstrates experience with business as well as fitness education.

✔ Obtain a personal-training certificate and certification in CPR.

✔ If you're working a lower-level job in a health facility, be upbeat, organized, responsible, and flexible. Display the qualities a good sport and fitness manager needs.

Career Connections

For further information on this field, contact these organizations.

American Association for Physical Activity and Recreation
http://www.aahperd.org

National Coalition for Promoting Physical Activity http://www.ncppa.org

National Recreation and Park Association http://www.nrpa.org (Click "Professional Development;" then select "Higher Education.")

The President's Council on Physical Fitness and Sports
http://www.fitness.gov

Associate's Degree Programs

Many colleges offer associate's degree and certificate programs in sports and fitness management. Here is a selection:

The University of Wisconsin-Parkside, College of Arts and Sciences, Kenosha, Wisconsin

Morrisville State College, Morrisville, New York

Lorain County Community College, Elyria, Ohio

Indian Hills Community College, Centerville, Iowa

Pima Community College, Tucson, Arizona

Financial Aid

Scholarships are available on the national level and from individual educational institutions. Refer to Appendix B for more information.

The **Bill Kane Undergraduate Scholarship** awards a $1,000 scholarship annually to an undergraduate health education major at an accredited college/university in the United States or a U.S. territory. http://www.aahperd.org/AAHE/template.cfm?template=heawards/AAH E.html

The **Ruth Abernathy Presidential Scholarship** (formerly the National Presidential Scholarship of AAHPERD). To find out more click on "Presidential Scholarship" on the "About AAHPERD" drop-down menu at http://www.aahperd.org.

Related Careers

Sports agent and business manager, coach and scout, fitness trainer and aerobics instructor, professional athlete, recreation worker, and umpire.

Appendix A

Tools for Career Success

When 20-year-old Justin Schulman started job-hunting for a position as a fitness trainer—his first step toward managing a fitness facility—he didn't mess around. "I immediately opened the Yellow Pages and started calling every number listed under health and fitness, inquiring about available positions," he recalls. Schulman's energy and enterprise paid off: He wound up with interviews that led to several offers of part-time work.

Schulman's experience highlights an essential lesson for jobseekers: There are plenty of opportunities out there, but jobs won't come to you—especially the career-oriented, well-paying ones that that you'll want to stick with over time. You've got to seek them out.

Uncover Your Interests

Whether you're in high school or bringing home a full-time paycheck, the first step toward landing your ideal job is assessing your interests. You need to figure out what makes you tick. After all, there is a far greater chance that you'll enjoy and succeed in a career that taps into your passions, inclinations, and natural abilities. That's what happened with career-changer Scott Rolfe. He was already 26 when he realized he no longer wanted to work in the food industry. "I'm an avid outdoorsman," Rolfe says, "and I have an appreciation for natural resources that many people take for granted." Rolfe turned his passions into his ideal job as a forest technician.

If you have a general idea of what your interests are, you're far ahead of the game. You may know that you're cut out for a health care career, for instance, or one in business. You can use a specific volume of *Top Careers in Two Years* to discover what position to target. If you are unsure of your direction, check out the whole range of volumes to see the scope of jobs available. Ask yourself, what job or jobs would I most like to do if I *already* had the training and skills? Then remind yourself that this is what your two-year training will accomplish.

You can also use interest inventories and skills-assessment programs to further pinpoint your ideal career. Your school or public librarian or guidance counselor should be able to help you locate such assessments. Web sites such as America's Career InfoNet (http://www.acinet.org) and JobWeb (http://www.jobweb.com) also offer interest inventories. Don't forget the help advisers at any two-year college can provide to target your interests. You'll find suggestions for Web sites related to specific careers at the end of each chapter in any *Top Careers in Two Years* volume.

Unlock Your Network

The next stop toward landing the perfect job is networking. The word may make you cringe. But networking isn't about putting on a suit, walking into a roomful of strangers, and pressing your business card on everyone. Networking is simply introducing yourself and exchanging job-related and other information that may prove helpful to one or both of you. That's what Susan Tinker-Muller did. Quite a few years ago, she struck up a conversation with a fellow passenger on her commuter train. Little did she know that the natural interest she expressed in the woman's accounts payable department would lead to news about a job opening there. Tinker-Muller's networking landed her an entry-level position in accounts payable with MTV Networks. She is now the accounts payable administrator.

Tinker-Muller's experience illustrates why networking is so important. Fully 80 percent of openings are *never* advertised, and more than half of all employees land their jobs through networking, according to the U.S. Bureau of Labor Statistics. That's 8 out of 10 jobs that you'll miss if you don't get out there and talk with people. And don't think you can bypass face-to-face conversations by posting your résumé on job sites like Monster.com and Hotjobs.com and then waiting for employers to contact you. That's so mid-1990s! Back then, tens of thousands, if not millions, of job seekers diligently posted their résumés on scores of sites. Then they sat back and waited . . . and waited . . . and waited. You get the idea. Big job sites like Monster and Hotjobs have their place, of course, but relying solely on an Internet job search is about as effective as throwing your résumé into a black hole.

Begin your networking efforts by making a list of people to talk to: teachers, classmates (and their parents), anyone you've worked with, neighbors, worship acquaintances, and anyone you've interned or volunteered with. You can also expand your networking opportunities through the student sections of industry associations (listed at the end of each chapter of *Top Careers in Two Years*); attending or volunteering at industry events, association conferences, career fairs; and through job-shadowing. Keep in mind that only rarely will any of the people on your list be in a position to offer you a job. But whether they know it or not, they probably know someone who knows someone who is. That's why your networking goal is not to ask for a job but the name of someone to talk with. Even when you network with an employer, it's wise to say something like, "You may not have any positions available, but might you know someone I could talk with to find out more about what it's like to work in this field?"

Also, keep in mind that networking is a two-way street. For instance, you may be talking with someone who has a job opening that isn't appropriate for you. If you can refer someone else to the employer, either person may well be disposed to help you someday in the future.

Dial-Up Help

Call your contacts directly, rather than e-mail them. (E-mails are too easy for busy people to ignore, even if they don't mean to.) Explain that you're a recent graduate in your field; that Mr. Jones referred you; and that you're wondering if you could stop by for 10 or 15 minutes at your contact's convenience to find out a little more about how the industry works. If you leave this message as a voicemail, note that you'll call back in a few days to follow up. If you reach your contact directly, expect that they'll say they're too busy at the moment to see you. Ask, "Would you mind if I check back in a couple of weeks?" Then jot down a note in your date book or set up a reminder in your computer calendar and call back when it's time. (Repeat this above scenario as needed, until you get a meeting.)

Once you have arranged to talk with someone in person, prep yourself. Scour industry publications for insightful articles; having up-to-date knowledge about industry trends shows your networking contacts that you're dedicated and focused. Then pull together questions about specific employers and suggestions that will set you apart from the job-hunting pack in your field. The more specific your questions (for instance, about one type of certification versus another), the more likely your contact will see you as an "insider," worthy of passing along to a potential employer. At the end of any networking meeting, ask for the name of someone else who might be able to help you further target your search.

Get a Lift

When you meet with a contact in person (as well as when you run into someone fleetingly), you need an "elevator speech." This is a summary of up to two minutes that introduces who you are, as well as your experience and goals. An elevator speech should be short enough to be delivered during an elevator ride with a potential employer from the ground level to a high floor. In it, it's helpful to show that 1) you know the business involved; 2) you know the company; 3) you're qualified (give your work and educational information); and 4) you're goal-oriented, dependable, and hardworking. You'll be surprised how much information you can include in two minutes. Practice this speech in front of a mirror until you have the key points down very well. It should sound natural though, and you should come across as friendly, confident, and assertive. Remember, good eye contact needs to be part of your presentation as well as your everyday approach when meeting prospective employers or leads.

Get Your Résumé Ready

In addition to your elevator speech, another essential job-hunting tool is your résumé. Basically, a résumé is a little snapshot of you in words, reduced to one 8½ x 11-inch sheet of paper (or, at most, two sheets). You need a résumé whether you're in high school, college, or the workforce, and whether you've never held a job or have had many.

At the top of your résumé should be your heading. This is your name, address, phone numbers, and your e-mail address, which can be a sticking point. E-mail addresses such as sillygirl@yahoo.com or drinkingbuddy @hotmail.com won't score you any points. In fact they're a turn-off. So if you dreamed up your address after a night on the town, maybe it's time to upgrade. (Similarly, these days potential employers often check Myspace sites, personal blogs, and Web pages. What's posted there has been known to cost candidates a job offer.)

The first section of your résumé is a concise Job Objective (e.g., "Entry-level agribusiness sales representative seeking a position with a leading dairy cooperative"). These days, with word-processing software, it's easy and smart to adapt your job objective to the position for which you're applying. An alternative way to start a résumé, which some recruiters prefer, is to re-work the Job Objective into a Professional Summary. A Professional Summary doesn't mention the position you're seeking, but instead focuses on your job strengths (e.g., "Entry-level agribusiness sales rep; strengths include background in feed, fertilizer, and related markets and ability to contribute as a member of a sales team"). Which is better? It's your call.

The body of a résumé typically starts with your Job Experience. This is a chronological list of the positions you've held (particularly the ones that will help you land the job you want). Remember: never, never any fudging. However, it is okay to include volunteer positions and internships on the chronological list, as long as they're noted for what they are.

Next comes your Education section. Note: It's acceptable to flip the order of your Education and Job Experience sections if you're still in high school or have gone straight to college and don't have significant work experience. Summarize the major courses in your degree area, any certifications you've achieved, relevant computer knowledge, special seminars, or other school-related experience that will distinguish you. Include your grade average if it's more than 3.0. Don't worry if you haven't finished your degree. Simply write that you're currently enrolled in your program (if you are).

In addition to these elements, other sections may include professional organizations you belong to and any work-related achievements, awards, or recognition you've received. Also, you can have a section for your interests, such as playing piano or soccer (and include any notable achievements regarding your interests, for instance, placed third in Midwest Regional Piano Competition). You should also note other special abilities, such as "Fluent in French" or "Designed own Web site." These sorts of activities will reflect well on you, whether or not they are job-related.

You can either include your references or simply note, "References upon Request." Be sure to ask your references permission to use their name and alert them to the fact that they may be contacted, before you include them on your résumé. For more information on résumé writing, check out Web sites such as http://www.resume.monster.com.

Craft Your Cover Letter

When you apply for a job either online or by mail, it's appropriate to include a cover letter. A cover letter lets you convey extra information about yourself that doesn't fit or isn't always appropriate in your résumé. For instance, in a cover letter, you can and should mention the name of anyone who referred you to the job. You can go into some detail about the reason you're a great match, given the job description. You also can address any questions that might be raised in the potential employer's mind (for instance, a gap in your résumé). Don't, however, ramble on. Your cover letter should stay focused on your goal: to offer a strong, positive impression of yourself and persuade the hiring manager that you're worth an interview. Your cover letter gives you a chance to stand out from the other applicants and sell yourself. In fact, 23 percent of hiring managers say a candidate's ability to relate his or her experience to the job at hand is a top hiring consideration, according to a Careerbuilder.com survey.

You can write a positive, yet concise cover letter in three paragraphs: An introduction containing the specifics of the job you're applying for; a summary of why you're a good fit for the position and what you can do for the company; and a closing with a request for an interview, contact information, and thanks. Remember to vary the structure and tone of your cover letter. For instance, don't begin every sentence with "I."

Ace Your Interview

Preparation is the key to acing any job interview. This starts with researching the company or organization you're interviewing with. Start with the firm, group, or agency's own Web site. Explore it thoroughly; read about their products and services, their history, and sales and marketing information.

Check out their news releases, links that they provide, and read up on or Google members of the management team to get an idea of what they may be looking for in their employees.

Sites such as http://www.hoovers.com enable you to research companies across many industries. Trade publications in any industry (such as *Food Industry News, Hotel Business,* and *Hospitality Technology*) are also available online or in hard copy at many college or public libraries. Don't forget to make a phone call to contacts you have in the organization to get an even better idea of the company culture.

Preparation goes beyond research, however. It includes practicing answers to common interview questions:

- ☞ *Tell me about yourself* (Don't talk about your favorite bands or your personal history; give a brief summary of your background and interest in the particular job area.)
- ☞ *Why do you want to work here?* (Here's where your research into the company comes into play; talk about the firm's strengths and products or services.)
- ☞ *Why should we hire you?* (Now is your chance to sell yourself as a dependable, trustworthy, effective employee.)
- ☞ *Why did you leave your last job?* (This is not a talk show. Keep your answer short; never bad-mouth a previous employer. You can always say something simply such as, "It wasn't a good fit, and I was ready for other opportunities.")

Rehearse your answers, but don't try to memorize them. Responses that are natural and spontaneous come across better. Trying to memorize exactly what you want to say is likely to both trip you up and make you sound robotic.

As for the actual interview, to break the ice, offer a few pleasant remarks about the day, a photo in the interviewer's office, or something else similar. Then, once the interview gets going, listen closely and answer the questions you're asked, versus making any other point that you want to convey. If you're unsure whether your answer was adequate, simply ask, "Did that answer the question?" Show respect, good energy, and enthusiasm, and be upbeat. Employers are looking for people who are enjoyable to be around, as well as good workers. Show that you have a positive attitude and can get along well with others by not bragging during the interview, overstating your experience, or giving the appearance of being too self-absorbed. Avoid one-word answers, but at the same time don't blather. If you're faced with a silence after giving your response, pause for a few seconds, and then ask, "Is there anything else you'd like me to add?" Never look at your watch or answer your cellphone during an interview.

Near the interview's end, the interviewer is likely to ask you if you have any questions. Make sure that you have a few prepared, for instance:

☞ *"Tell me about the production process."*

☞ *"What's your biggest short-term challenge?"*

☞ *"How have recent business trends affected the company?"*

☞ *"Is there anything else that I can provide you with to help you make your decision?"*

☞ *"When will you make your hiring decision?"*

During a first interview, never ask questions like, "What's the pay?" "What are the benefits?" or "How much vacation time will I get?"

Find the Right Look

Appropriate dressing and grooming is also essential to interviewing success. For business jobs and many other occupations, it's appropriate to come to an interview in a nice (not stuffy) suit. However, different fields have various dress codes. In the music business, for instance, "business casual" reigns for many jobs. This is a slightly modified look, where slacks and a jacket are just fine for a guy, and a nice skirt and blouse and jacket or sweater are acceptable for a woman. Dressing overly "cool" will usually backfire.

In general, watch all of the basics from the shoes on up (no sneakers or sandals, and no overly high heels or short skirts for women). Also avoid attention-getting necklines, girls. Keep jewelry and other "bling" to a minimum. Tattoos and body jewelry are becoming more acceptable, but if you can take out piercings (other than in your ear), you're better off. Similarly, unusual hairstyles or colors may bias an employer against you, rightly or wrongly. Make sure your hair is neat and acceptable (get a haircut?). Also go light on the makeup, self-tanning products, body scents, and other grooming agents. Don't wear a baseball cap or any other type of hat; and by all means, take off your sunglasses!

Beyond your physical appearance, you already know to be well bathed to minimize odor (leave your home early if you tend to sweat, so you can cool off in private), make good eye contact, smile, speak clearly using proper English, use good posture (don't slouch), offer a firm handshake, and arrive within five minutes of your interview. (If you're unsure of where you're going, "Mapquest" it and consider making a dry-run to the site so you won't be late.) First impressions can make or break your interview.

Remember Follow-Up

After your interview, send a thank you note. This thoughtful gesture will separate you from most of the other candidates. It demonstrates your ability to follow through, and it catches your prospective employer's attention one more time. In a 2005 Careerbuilder.com survey, nearly 15 percent of 650 hiring managers said they wouldn't hire someone who failed to send a thank you letter after the interview. Thirty-two percent say they would still consider the candidate, but would think less of him or her.

So do you hand write or e-mail the thank you letter? The fact is that format preferences vary. One in four hiring managers prefer to receive a thank you note in e-mail form only; 19 percent want the e-mail, followed up with a hard copy; 21 percent want a typed hard-copy only; and 23 percent prefer just a handwritten note. (Try to check with an assistant on the format your potential employer prefers.) Otherwise, sending an e-mail and a handwritten copy is a safe way to proceed.

Winning an Offer

There are no sweeter words to a job hunter than, "We'd like to hire you." So naturally, when you hear them, you may be tempted to jump at the offer. *Don't.* Once an employer wants you, he or she will usually give you some time to make your decision and get any questions you may have answered. Now is the time to get specific about salary and benefits, and negotiate some of these points. If you haven't already done so, check out salary ranges for your position and area of the country on sites such as Payscale.com, Salary.com, and Salaryexpert.com (basic info is free; specific requests are not). Also, find out what sorts of benefits similar jobs offer. Then don't be afraid to negotiate in a diplomatic way. Asking for better terms is reasonable and expected. You may worry that asking the employer to bump up his offer may jeopardize your job, but handled intelligently, negotiating for yourself in fact may be a way to impress your future employer—and get a better deal for yourself.

After you've done all the hard work that successful job-hunting requires, you may be tempted to put your initiative into autodrive. However, the efforts you made to land your job-from clear communication to enthusiasm-are necessary now to pave your way to continued success. As Danielle Little, a human-resources assistant, says, "You must be enthusiastic and take the initiative. There is an urgency to prove yourself and show that you are capable of performing any and all related tasks. If your manager notices that you have potential, you will be given additional responsibilities, which will help advance your career." So do your best work on the job, and build your credibility. Your payoff will be career advancement and increased earnings.

Appendix B

Financial Aid

One major advantage of earning a two-year degree is that it is much less expensive than paying for a four-year school. Two years is naturally going to cost less than four, and two-year graduates enter the workplace and start earning a paycheck sooner than their four-year counterparts.

The latest statistics from the College Board show that average yearly total tuition and fees at a public two-year college is $2,191, compared to $5,491 at a four-year public college. That cost leaps to more than $21,000 on average for a year at a private four-year school.

With college costs relatively low, some two-year students overlook the idea of applying for financial aid at all. But the fact is, college dollars are available whether you're going to a trade school, community college, or university. About a third of all Pell Grants go to two-year public school students, and while two-year students receive a much smaller percentage of other aid programs, the funding is there for many who apply.

How Does Aid Work?

Financial aid comes in two basic forms: merit-based and need-based.

Merit-based awards are typically funds that recognize a particular talent or quality you may have, and they are given by private organizations, colleges, and the government. Merit-based awards range from scholarships for good writing to prizes for those who have shown promise in engineering. There are thousands of scholarships available for students who shine in academics, music, art, science, and more. Resources on how to get these awards are provided later in this chapter.

Need-based awards are given according to your ability to pay for college. In general, students from families that have less income and fewer assets receive more financial aid. To decide how much of this aid you qualify for, schools look at your family's income, assets, and other information regarding your finances. You provide this information on a financial aid form—usually the federal government's Free Application for Federal Student Aid (FAFSA). Based on the financial details you provide, the school of your choice calculates your Expected Family Contribution (EFC). This is the amount you are expected to pay toward your education each year.

Once your EFC is determined, a school uses this simple formula to figure out your financial aid package:

Cost of attendance at the school

- – **Your EFC**
- – **Other outside aid (private scholarships)**
- = **Need**

Schools put together aid packages that meet that need using loans, work-study, and grants.

Know Your School

When applying to a school, it's a good idea to find out their financial aid policy and history. Read over the school literature or contact the financial aid office and find out the following:

✔ *Is the school accredited?* Schools that are not accredited usually do not offer as much financial aid and are not eligible for federal programs.

✔ *What is the average financial aid package at the school?* The typical award size may influence your decision to apply or not.

✔ *What are all the types of assistance available?* Check if the school offers federal, state, private, or institutional aid.

✔ *What is the school's loan default rate?* The default rate is the percentage of students who took out federal student loans and failed to repay them on time. Schools that have a high default rate are often not allowed to offer certain federal aid programs.

✔ *What are the procedures and deadlines for submitting financial aid?* Policies can differ from school to school.

✔ *What is the school's definition of satisfactory academic progress?* To receive financial aid, you have to maintain your academic performance. A school may specify that you keep up at least a C+ or B average to keep getting funding.

✔ *What is the school's job placement rate?* The job placement rate is the percentage of students who find work in their field of study after graduating.

You'll want a school with a good placement rate so you can earn a good salary that may help you pay back any student loans you have.

Be In It to Win It

The key to getting the most financial aid possible is filling out the forms, and you have nothing to lose by applying. Most schools require that you file the FAFSA, which is *free* to submit, and you can even do it online. For more information on the FAFSA, visit the Web site at http://www.fafsa.ed.gov. If you have any trouble with the form, you can call 1-800-4-FED-AID for help.

To receive aid using the FAFSA, you must submit the form soon after January 1 prior to the start of your school year. A lot of financial aid is delivered on a first-come, first-served basis, so be sure to apply on time.

Filing for aid will require some work to gather your financial information. You'll need details regarding your assets and from your income tax forms, which include the value of all your bank accounts and investments. The form also asks if you have other siblings in college, the age of your parents, or if you have children. These factors can determine how much aid you receive.

Three to four weeks after you submit the FAFSA, you receive a document called the Student Aid Report (SAR). The SAR lists all the information you provided in the FAFSA and tells you how much you'll be expected to contribute toward school, or your Expected Family Contribution (EFC). It's important to review the information on the SAR carefully and make any corrections right away. If there are errors on this document, it can affect how much financial aid you'll receive.

The Financial Aid Package

Using information on your SAR, the school of your choice calculates your need (as described earlier) and puts together a financial aid package. Aid packages are often built with a combination of loans, grants, and work-study. You may also have won private scholarships that will help reduce your costs.

Keep in mind that aid awarded in the form of loans has to be paid back with interest just like a car loan. If you don't pay back according to agreed upon terms, you can go into *default*. Default usually occurs if you've missed payments for 180 days. Defaulted loans are often sent to collection agencies, which can charge costly fees and even take money owed out of your wages. Even worse, a defaulted loan is a strike on your credit history. If you have a negative credit history, lenders may deny you a mortgage, car loan, or other personal loan. There's also financial incentive for paying back on time— many lenders will give a 1 percent discount or more for students who make consecutive timely payments. The key is not to borrow more than you can afford. Know exactly how much your monthly payments will be on a loan when it comes due and estimate if those monthly payments will fit in your future budget. If you ever do run into trouble with loan payments, don't hesitate to contact your lender and see if you can come up with a new payment arrangement—lenders want to help you pay rather than see you go into default. If you have more than one loan, look into loan consolidation, which can lower overall monthly payments and sometimes lock in interest rates that are relatively low.

The Four Major Sources of Aid

U.S. Government Financial Aid

The federal government is the biggest source of financial aid. To find all about federal aid programs, visit http://www.studentaid.fed.gov or call 1-800-4-FED-AID with any questions. Download the free brochure *Funding Education Beyond High School,* which tells you all the details on federal programs. To get aid from federal programs you must be a regular student working toward a degree or certificate in an eligible program. You also have to have a high school diploma or equivalent, be a U.S. citizen or eligible noncitizen and have a valid Social Security number (check http://www.ssa.gov for info). If you are a male aged 18–25, you have to register for the Selective Service. (Find out more about that requirement at http://www.sss.gov or call 1-847-688-6888.) You must also certify that you are not in default on a student loan and that you will use your federal aid only for educational purposes.

Some specifics concerning federal aid programs can change a little each year, but the major programs are listed here and the fundamentals stay the same from year to year. (Note that amounts you receive generally depend on your enrollment status—whether it be full-time or part-time.)

Pell Grant
For students demonstrating significant need, this award has been ranging between $400 and $4,050. The size of a Pell grant does not depend on how much other aid you receive.

Supplemental Educational Opportunity Grant (SEOG)
Again for students with significant need, this award ranges from $100 to $4,000 a year. The size of the SEOG can be reduced according to how much other aid you receive.

Work-Study
The Federal Work-Study Program provides jobs for students showing financial need. The program encourages community service and work related to a student's course of study. You earn at least minimum wage and are paid at least once a month. Again, funds must be used for educational expenses.

Perkins Loans

With a low interest rate of 5 percent, this program lets students who can document the need borrow up to $4,000 a year.

Stafford Loans

These loans are available to all students regardless of need. However, students with need receive *subsidized* Staffords, which do not accrue interest while you're in school or in deferment. Students without need can take *unsubsidized* Staffords, which do accrue interest while you are in school or in deferment. Interest rates vary but can go no higher than 8.25 percent. Loan amounts vary too, according to what year of study you're in and whether you are financially dependent on your parents or not. Students defined as independent of their parents can borrow much more. (Students who have their own kids are also defined as independent. Check the exact qualifications for independent and dependent status on the federal government Web site http://www.studentaid.fed.gov.)

PLUS Loans

These loans for parents of dependent students are also available regardless of need. Parents with good credit can borrow up to the cost of attendance minus any other aid received. Interest rates are variable but can go no higher than 9 percent.

Tax Credits

Depending on your family income, qualified students can take federal tax deductions for education with maximums ranging from $1,500 to $2,000.

AmeriCorps

This program provides full-time educational awards in return for community service work. You can work before, during, or after your postsecondary education and use the funds either to pay current educational expenses or to repay federal student loans. Americorps participants work assisting teachers in Head Start, helping on conservation projects, building houses for the homeless, and doing other good works. For more information, visit http://www.AmeriCorps.gov

State Financial Aid

All states offer financial aid, both merit-based and need-based. Most states use the FAFSA to determine eligibility, but you'll have to contact your state's higher education agency to find out the exact requirements. You can get contact information for your state at http://www.bcol02.ed.gov/Programs/EROD/org_list.cfm. Most of the state aid programs are available only if you study at a school in the state where you reside. Some states are very generous, especially if you're attending a state college or university. California's Cal Grant program gives needy state residents free tuition at in-state public universities.

School-Sponsored Financial Aid

The school you attend may offer its own loans, grants, and work programs. Many have academic- or talent-based scholarships for top-performing students. Some two-year programs offer cooperative education opportunities where you combine classroom study with off-campus work related to your major. The work gives you hands-on experience and some income, ranging from $2,500 to $15,000 per year depending on the program. Communicate with your school's financial aid department and make sure you're applying for the most aid you can possibly get.

Private Scholarships

While scholarships for students heading to four-year schools may be more plentiful, there are awards for the two-year students. Scholarships reward students for all sorts of talent—academic, artistic, athletic, technical, scientific, and more. You have to invest time hunting for the awards that you might qualify for. The Internet now offers many great scholarship search services. Some of the best ones are:

The College Board (http://www.collegeboard.com/pay)

FastWeb! (http://www.fastweb.monster.com)

MACH25 (http://www.collegenet.com)

Scholarship Research Network (http://www.srnexpress.com)

SallieMae's College Answer (http://www.collegeanswer.com)

Note: Be careful of scholarship-scam services that charge a fee for finding you awards but end up giving you nothing more than a few leads that you could have gotten for free with a little research on your own. Check out the Federal Trade Commission's Project ScholarScam (http://www.ftc.gov/bcp/conline/edcams/scholarship).

In your hunt for scholarship dollars, be sure to look into local community organizations (the Elks Club, Lions Club, PTA, etc.), local corporations, employers (your employer or your parents' may offer tuition assistance), trade groups, professional associations (National Electrical Contractors Association, etc.), clubs (Boy Scouts, Girl Scouts, Distributive Education Club of America, etc.), heritage organizations (Italian, Japanese,

Chinese, and other groups related to ethnic origin), church groups, and minority assistance programs.

Once you find awards you qualify for, you have to put in the time applying. This usually means filling out an application, writing a personal statement, and gathering recommendations.

General Scholarships

A few general scholarships for students earning two-year degrees are

Coca-Cola Scholars Foundation, Inc.
Coca-Cola offers 350 thousand-dollar scholarships (http://www.coca colascholars.org) per year specifically for students attending two-year institutions.

Phi Theta Kappa (PTK)
This organization is the International Honor Society of the Two-Year College. PTK is one of the sponsors of the All-USA Academic Team program, which annually recognizes 60 outstanding two-year college students (http://scholarships.ptk.org). First, Second, and Third Teams, each consisting of 20 members, are selected. The 20 First Team members receive stipends of $2,500 each. All 60 members of the All-USA Academic Team and their colleges receive extensive national recognition through coverage in *USA TODAY*. There are other great scholarships for two-year students listed on this Web site.

Hispanic Scholarship Fund (HSF)
HSF's High School Scholarship Program (http://www.hsf.net/scholar ship/programs/hs.php) is designed to assist high school students of Hispanic heritage obtain a college degree. It is available to graduating high school seniors who plan to enroll full-time at a community college during the upcoming academic year. Award amounts range from $1,000 to $2,500.

The Military
All branches of the military offer tuition dollars in exchange for military service. You have to decide if military service is for you. The Web site http://www.myfuture.com attempts to answer any questions you might have about military service.

Lower Your Costs

In addition to getting financial aid, you can reduce college expenses by being a money-smart student. Here are some tips.

Use Your Campus

Schools offer perks that some students never take advantage of. Use the gym. Take in a school-supported concert or movie night. Attend meetings and lectures with free refreshments.

Flash Your Student ID

Students often get discounts at movies, museums, restaurants, and stores. Always be sure to ask if there is a lower price for students and carry your student ID with you at all times. You can often save 10 to 20 percent on purchases.

Budget Your Funds

Writing a budget of your income and expenses can help you be a smart spender. Track what you buy on a budget chart. This awareness will save you dollars.

Share Rides

Commuting to school or traveling back to your hometown? Check and post on student bulletin boards for ride shares.

Buy Used Books

Used textbooks can cost half as much as new. Check your campus bookstore for deals and also try http://www.eCampus.com and http://www.bookcentral.com

Put Your Credit Card in the Freezer

That's what one student did to stop overspending. You can lock your card away any way you like, just try living without the ease of credit for awhile. You'll be surprised at the savings.

A Two-Year Student's Financial Aid Package

Minnesota State Colleges and Universities provides this example of how a two-year student pays for college. Note how financial aid reduces his out-of-pocket cost to about $7,000 per year.

Jeremy's Costs for One Year

Jeremy is a freshman at a two-year college in the Minnesota. He has a sister in college, and his parents own a home but have no other significant savings. His family's income: $42,000.

College Costs for One Year

Tuition	$3,437
Fees	$388
Estimated room and board*	$7,200
Estimated living expenses**	$6,116
Total cost of attendance	*$17,141*

Jeremy's Financial Aid

Federal grants (does not require repayment)	$2,800
Minnesota grant (does not require repayment)	$676
Work-study earnings	$4,000
Student loan (requires repayment)	$2,625
Total financial aid	*$10,101*

Total cost to Jeremy's family	*$7,040*

* Estimated cost reflecting apartment rent rate and food costs. The estimates are used to calculate the financial aid. If a student lives at home with his or her parents, the actual cost could be much less, although the financial aid amounts may remain the same.

** This is an estimate of expenses including transportation, books, clothing, and social activities.

Index